IS-360: Preparing for Mass Casualty Incidents

By

Fema

6/24/2013

IS-360 - Preparing for Mass Casualty Incidents: A Guide for Schools, Higher Education, and Houses of Worship

Lesson 1: Are You Prepared

Thinking About the Unthinkable

Too many communities have been touched by armed violence. Sandy Hook, Columbine, Virginia Tech, New Life Church—each time such an event happens in another community, it touches us as a Nation and we are reminded that it could happen in our own community.

Mass casualty incidents may occur wherever people congregate—in elementary and secondary schools, on college campuses, in houses of worship, or in other venues. They are part of a complex problem that affects the entire community, and that will require the whole community, working together, to address.

While no measures can ensure absolute security, there are ways we can significantly reduce the risk. Many planned attacks have been averted and countless lives have been saved by being prepared. By sharing our collective insights, expertise, and effort, we can minimize the likelihood that such events will take place and be prepared to act if an incident does occur.

Are you prepared?

This course will help you understand the threats and challenges of mass casualty incidents, and present ways you can improve your level of preparedness should the unthinkable occur.

Course Overview

This course provides leading practices and resources to assist elementary and secondary schools, institutions of higher education, and houses of worship in developing emergency plans for preparing for, responding to, and recovering from mass casualty incidents.

After completing this course, you should be able to identify key considerations and strategies for preparing for mass casualty incidents, including:

- Understanding the threats and challenges.
- Establishing planning processes.
- Assessing and mitigating vulnerabilities.
- Establishing response procedures.
- Planning for recovery.
- Staying prepared.

Lesson Overview

After completing this lesson you should be able to identify:

- The threats and challenges associated with mass casualty incidents in schools, institutions of higher education, and houses of worship.
- Lessons learned from past mass casualty incidents.
- The role of the whole community in preventing, protecting, and mitigating against active shooter/mass casualty threats.
- Key factors from incidents where communities were able to prevent an active shooter incident or mitigate mass casualties.

What Is the Threat?

K-12 School: In 1998 at Westside Middle School in Jonesboro, Arkansas, an 11-year-old boy asked to be excused from his class. Upon leaving the classroom he pulled a fire alarm and ran outside. As the teachers and students evacuated the building, he and another boy opened fire. They killed five people and wounded 10 others. The boys were caught with a stockpile of firearms, ammunition, and other weapons.

Institution of Higher Education: Early one morning in 2007, a university student at Virginia Tech started a deadly shooting spree, first killing a female student and a residential advisor in a dormitory building. He then continued his spree about 2½ hours later in a lecture building, where he shot and killed 5 faculty members and 27 students and injured 17.

House of Worship: One Sunday in 2012, a man with a history of extremist group involvement began a shooting rampage outside a house of worship in Oak Creek, Wisconsin. He then entered the building and continued firing. He ultimately took the lives of six people and injured three others, before killing himself after exchanging gunfire with police officers.

As these examples illustrate, there is no single scenario for mass casualty incidents. Attacks vary in where they happen, who the victims are, how many assailants are involved, what weapons are used, and how they are carried out.

What they do have in common is the shock, the violence, the loss of life, and the terrible impact on the community. These events are the unthinkable.

Terminology

Various terms are used to describe such incidents—*armed assault, armed attack, intrusion, deadly force incident, active shooter, mass casualty incident,* and *targeted act of violence* to name a few.

An **active shooter** is an individual actively engaged in killing or attempting to kill people in a confined space or other populated area, most often using firearms and following no pattern or method in the selection of victims.

Targeted violence refers to any incident of violence where the location was deliberately selected and not simply a random site of opportunity and where the perpetrator selected a target before the incident. For example, incidents where the attack "just happened to occur" at that location, such as consequences of gang or drug activity, would not be included.

How Great Is the Threat?

Incidents of this type invariably receive intense and extended media coverage, giving them a very high profile. However, despite the attention given to isolated instances of extreme violence, the chances of this type of incident occurring in educational facilities and houses of worship is actually quite low, and the odds against such an attack occurring in any particular location are enormous.

For example, according to the U.S. Secret Service and U.S. Department of Education, the odds are one in 1 million that a student will die at school as a result of a violent act.

Scope of the Threat

Elementary-Secondary Schools:

- Relative to the risk of violent victimization that children face outside of school, the risk they face in school is minimal. During the 2009-2010 school year, more than 49 million students were enrolled in prekindergarten through 12th grade.

During this period there were 17 school homicides (less than 2 percent of the total number of youth homicides).

- The U.S. Secret Service and the U.S. Department of Education identified 37 incidents of targeted school-based attacks, committed by 41 individuals, over the 25-year period from 1974 to 2000.

Institutions of Higher Education:

A study of targeted violence affecting institutions of higher education made the following observations:

- In the 2006-07 school year (the year in which the attack at Virginia Tech occurred), there were 6,563 postsecondary institutions in the United States, with student enrollment of 17.8 million.
- During this period, 0.1 percent of reported campus crimes were murders and non-negligent manslaughter.
- During the period 2000-2008, there were 83 instances of targeted violence.

Houses of Worship:

- A 2010 U.S. religious census reported 344,894 congregations in 236 religious groups with 150,686,156 adherents. According to the Pew Research Center, 39 percent of the population self-reported that they attend a place of worship at least once a week.
- In the past 10 years, there have been more than 600 acts of violence committed in houses of worship.

Definitions

Risk: The potential for an unwanted outcome resulting from an incident, event, or occurrence, as determined by its likelihood and the associated consequences.

Threat: A natural or manmade occurrence, individual, entity, or action that has or indicates the potential to harm life, information, operations, the environment, and/or property.

Vulnerability: A physical feature or operational attribute that renders an entity open to exploitation or susceptible to a given hazard.

Why Prepare?

If the odds of such incidents in any given educational or worship setting are so low, why invest in preparing for them?

The impact of targeted attacks cannot be measured in statistics alone. Schools and places of worship traditionally are places of safety and peace where people can learn and worship without fear of armed violence.

However, violence can happen in any setting, and each attack—no matter how rare—can result in many fatalities. Even one such death will have a tremendous and lasting effect on family and loved ones, the surrounding community, and the Nation as a whole and can generate tremendous stress and anxiety.

Properly addressing this type of risk can help to reinforce a sense of safety for people who work at, attend, or worship in these normally peaceful settings.

Past Incidents

Numerous studies have documented and analyzed past incidents to identify contributing factors and strategies that may help in preventing such attacks, mitigating the casualties, effectively responding, and recovering after the event.

Incidents in K-12 Schools

Incident Place	Incident Date	Brief Description
Cleveland Elementary School, Stockton, California	January 17, 1989	A man (age 24) set his car on fire in the parking lot of Cleveland Elementary School and then entered the school grounds and began shooting. He killed five students, and wounded 29 students and one teacher. He fired approximately 106 shots in 2 minutes and then shot himself in the head with a pistol.
Lindhurst High School, Olivehurst, California	May 1, 1992	A former student (age 20) of Lindhurst High School held students and teachers hostage. He shot and killed three students and one teacher before surrendering to police.
Westside Middle School, Jonesboro, Arkansas	March 24, 1998	Two boys (ages 11 and 13) gathered weapons in a van and then drove to Westside Middle School. Once at school, one boy entered the school and pulled a fire alarm and went outside to join other boy. As teachers and students evacuated the building, the boys opened fire, killing four students and one teacher and wounding 10 others. The boys

		then ran into the woods and were caught by police.
Thurston High School, Springfield, Oregon	May 20-21, 1998	A teenage boy (age 15) began his killing spree at home killing his father and mother. The following morning he drove to his high school armed with multiple weapons. He entered the school and walked down a hallway shooting at students. He shot 27 students, killing two before being tackled by students when he tried to reload.
Columbine High School, Littleton, Colorado	April 20, 1999	Two high school students (ages 17 and 18) entered Columbine High School and placed 2 propane bombs in the cafeteria and then waited in their cars for the bombs to detonate. When the bombs failed to detonate they approached the school armed with guns and a large amount of ammunition. They began shooting students outside the school and continued shooting inside and randomly throwing small improvised explosive devices. They killed 13 people and injured 23. The spree ended when the two committed suicide.
Red Lake Senior High School, Red Lake, Minnesota	March 21, 2005	A 16-year-old high school student killed his grandfather (a tribal police officer) and companion in their home. He took his grandfather's service pistol, police shotgun, and body armor and drove his police car to Red Lake High School. He shot and killed an unarmed security guard who tried to subdue him and then killed a teacher and five students, all within 3 minutes. After being wounded in an exchange of gunfire with tribal police, he killed himself at the school.
Amish Schoolhouse, Nickel Mines, Pennsylvania	October 2, 2006	A milk truck driver (age 32) entered a one-room Amish school house armed with three guns. He sent the boys and adults outside and then opened fire on the girls, killing five and critically wounding five. He killed himself when police arrived at the school.
Heath High School, West Paducah, Kentucky	December 1, 2007	A 14-year-old student at Heath High School fired on a school prayer group, killing three students. After firing several shots the

		shooter stopped, put the gun down, and surrendered to the principal.
Chardon High School, Chardon Ohio	February 27, 2012	A 17-year-old boy entered the cafeteria of Chardon High School and opened fire, killing three students and wounding two others. The assailant was arrested outside the school.
Sandy Hook Elementary School, Newtown, Connecticut	December 14, 2012	A man (age 20) shot and killed his mother in her home. He then then drove to Sandy Hook Elementary School where he forced his way into the school and opened fire. He killed a 26 people, including 20 students ages six and seven. He then killed himself as police closed in on him.

Incidents in Houses of Worship

Incident Place	Incident Date	Brief Description
Wedgwood Baptist Church, Fort Worth, Texas	September 15, 1999	A 47-year-old man entered a church during a teen rally and began shooting. He killed seven people, including three teenagers, and injured seven people. He threw a pipe bomb into the church and then killed himself.
Living Church of God, Brookfield, Wisconsin	March 12, 2005	A 44-year-old man killed seven people at a church meeting held at a hotel. He killed the pastor, the pastor's 16-year-old son, and himself and injured four others.
Ministry of Jesus Christ, Baton Rouge, Louisiana	May 21, 2006	A 25-year-old man entered the church and fired at congregants during the Sunday service. After killing four people and wounding the pastor, he fled in a car with his wife and three children. He was later captured at a nearby apartment complex.
First Congregational Church, Neosho, Missouri	August 12, 2007	A 52-year-old man killed the pastor and two deacons, and wounded five others in the church.
New Life Church, Colorado Springs, Colorado	December 9, 2007	A 24-year-old former member of the Youth With a Mission in Arvada, CO, attacked the mission, killing two people. Thirteen hours later he opened fire at the New Life Church, where he killed two women. The gunman

		was shot several times by an off-duty security officer but ultimately killed himself.
Tennessee Valley Unitarian Universalist Church, Knoxville, Tennessee	July 27, 2008	A 58-year-old man entered a church during a children's performance and used a shotgun to kill two people. He was stopped and restrained by church members until the police arrived.
St. Thomas Syrian Orthodox Church, Clifton, New Jersye	November 23, 2008	A man entered a church where he shot and killed his estranged wife and another congregant who tried to intervene, and wounded another.
First Baptist Church, Maryville, Illinois	March 8, 2009	A 27-year-old man entered a church armed with a gun, ammunition, and a knife. He first shot the pastor. When the gun jammed, he pulled out a knife and stabbed two congregants who tried to subdue him. He had marked the day of his attack in his calendar as "death day."
Sikh Temple of Wisconsin, Oak Creek, Wisconsin	August 5, 2012	A 40-year-old man opened fire in the parking lot of the Sikh Temple of Wisconsin and then entered the building shooting congregants. He killed six people and injured three and then, in a gunfire exchange with police officers, killed himself.

Incidents in Institutions of Higher Education

Incident Place	**Incident Date**	**Brief Description**
University of Iowa, Iowa City, Iowa	November 1, 1991	A 28-year-old graduate student shot and killed four people and injured two more in a shooting at the university. He then killed himself.
University of Arizona, Tucson, Arizona	October 28, 2002	A 41-year-old nursing student shot and killed three of his professors and then killed himself.
Appalachian School of Law, Grundy, Virginia	January 16, 2002	A 42-year-old student who was on the verge of suspension shot and killed the school's dean, a professor, and a student and injured three other students.

Virginia Polytechnic Institute and State University, Blacksburg, Virginia	April 16, 2007	A 23-year-old student entered a dormitory and shot and killed two students. After returning to his dormitory to change his clothes, he then continued his killing spree in classrooms, where he killed 30 people, injured 17, and killed himself.
Delaware State University, Dover, Delaware	September 21, 2007	An 18-year-old student shot two other students after an argument in the cafeteria, one of whom died later. The perpetrator was arrested in his dormitory.
Northern Illinois University, DeKalb, Illinois	February 14, 2008	A 27-year-old graduate student entered a lecture hall and began firing on a class with 162 people. He killed 5 students and injured 17, then took his own life.
Louisiana Technical College, Baton Rouge, Louisiana	February 8, 2008	A 23-year-old nursing student opened fire in a classroom. She shot and killed two other students and then killed herself.
University of Alabama in Huntsville, Huntsville, Alabama	February 12, 2010	A 44-year-old professor shot and killed three professors and injured three others during a faculty meeting.
Oikos University, Oakland, California	April 2, 2012	An expelled 43-year-old student entered the school in search of an administrator and began shooting when she was not there. The gunman killed seven people and injured three others. He later surrendered to police several miles from the school.

Note: This list is not all-inclusive.

What Have We Learned From Past Incidents?

Incidents come in many varieties and unfold in different ways. However, according to the findings of the Safe School Initiative, past incidents do share some common characteristics that can help you understand and be ready in the unlikely event that an incident occurs at your site.

This section of the lesson will summarize key lessons from that study. Although the study focused on incidents in schools, the findings can generally be applied to other venues.

No Single Assailant Profile

There is no single profile or stereotype of the assailants or their motivations. The attackers varied substantially in personality, social characteristics, background, age, home situation, mental health history, prior encounters with law enforcement, and other factors.

Profiling on the basis of these factors, therefore, is not effective for identifying those who may pose a risk for targeted violence. It is much more productive to focus on **behaviors and communications**—warning signs that someone might be planning or preparing for an attack.

Warning Signs Are Common

Most attackers engaged in some troubling behaviors prior to the incident that caused concern or indicated a need for help. Such behaviors included:

- Research, planning, and preparation (for example, researching how to build a bomb, sketching maps and diagrams, trying to obtain a gun).
- Suicidal threats and attempts.
- Difficulty coping with significant losses or personal failures such as death of a loved one, loss of status, job loss, divorce, or academic failure.
- History of being bullied, threatened, harassed, or attacked by others.
- Inappropriate interest in accounts of mass violence, or violent themes in movies, books, video games, or their own writings.

Attackers Make Plans

Incidents of targeted violence are rarely impulsive. In almost all incidents, the attacker developed the idea to harm the target before the attack. In many cases, the person formulated the idea for the attack at least 2 weeks in advance and planned out the incident.

Targeted violence is typically the end result of an understandable, often discernible, process of thinking and behavior.

Example—Virginia Tech: The student responsible for killing at least 30 people at Virginia Tech appeared to have planned his attack for weeks—purchasing weapons, testing campus security, and preparing documentation.

Virginia Polytechnic Institute and State University, April 2007

The student responsible for killing at least 30 people at Virginia Tech, had showed signs of disturbing behavior before his attack. He was removed from class for disturbing other students, tutored separately for another class, and encouraged by a faculty member to get counseling. He was accused twice of stalking female students, although charges were not filed. He also made a suicidal statement to his suitemate and was taken to a psychiatric hospital.

On April 16, 2007, the school gunman began his shooting spree by killing two students in a dormitory around 7 a.m. and then continuing his attack in a classroom building around 9:45 a.m. After killing 30 people and injuring numerous others, he ended his attack by shooting himself.

Evidence found in the gunman's dorm room indicated that he planned the assault well in advance. He purchased his first handgun 5 weeks prior to the attack and then waited the required 30 days before purchasing his second handgun. Also the week before, he may have issued bomb threats against the engineering buildings to test campus security, and sometime in advance he prepared a package of videos, photos, and a rambling document that he mailed to NBC News in New York in between his shootings.

Attackers Talk About Their Plans

Most attackers didn't threaten their targets directly before the attack. But prior to most incidents, the attacker told someone—a friend, schoolmate, sibling—and sometimes many people, about the idea or plan before taking action.

In nearly every case of school attacks, the person who was told was a peer and rarely did anything to bring the information to an adult's attention. In fact, in many cases, friends or fellow students actually encouraged the attacker to act.

The U.S. Department of Education and the U.S. Secret Service researched this dynamic and identified strategies that will increase the chances that people who have information will come forward.

Peer Involvement

In one incident, for example, the attacker had planned to shoot students in the lobby of his school prior to the beginning of the school day. He told two friends exactly what he had planned and asked three others to meet him that morning in the mezzanine overlooking the lobby, ostensibly so that these students would be out of harm's way.

On most mornings, usually only a few students would congregate on the mezzanine before the school day began. However, by the time the attacker arrived at school on the morning of the attack, word about what was going to happen had spread to such an extent that 24 students were on the mezzanine waiting for the attack to begin. One student who knew the attack was to occur brought a camera so that he could take pictures of the event.

Attackers Often Have Easy Access to Weapons

In past incidents, most attackers had used guns previously and had access to guns. In nearly two-thirds of school incidents, for example, the attackers obtained the weapons from their own home or that of a relative.

Remember, however, that although guns have been the weapon of choice in many incidents, it is unwise to focus only on "active shooter" scenarios. Past assailants have used guns, knives, improvised explosive devices, fire, and other types of weapons, and they have used firearms and explosives in combination. Future attackers could very well expand their methods to include weapons of terror not seen in past incidents.

Example—Westside Middle School: The two middle school boys who shot their classmates and teachers in Jonesboro, Arkansas, in 1998 as they evacuated the school were caught with 10 to 13 (sources vary) fully loaded firearms, 200 rounds of ammunition, a crossbow, and several hunting knives. All of the weapons belonged to the family of one of the boys.

Westside Middle School, March 1998

Two boys ages 11 and 13 gathered weapons in a van and drove to Westside Middle School. Once at school, one boy pulled a fire alarm and then joined his friend outside. As teachers and students evacuated the building, the boys opened fire, killing four students and one teacher and wounding 10 others. The boys then ran into the woods and surrendered when they were challenged by armed police officers.

They were found with 10 to 13 fully loaded firearms, 200 rounds of ammunition, a crossbow, and hunting knives. All of the weapons were owned by one of the boy's family. The boys were experienced shooters who belonged to gun clubs and participated in shooting competitions.

Both had expressed hostility toward others and threatened something big was going to happen. One had overt disciplinary problems, while the other was described as well-mannered and cheerful, although he had fired his BB gun at children and animals.

The two were convicted as juveniles with the maximum penalty under State law, and then convicted of the Federal crime of bringing a gun to school. They were released from prison in 2005 and 2007.

Law Enforcement May Not Be the First To Respond

Most incidents last 20 minutes or less. Even when emergency personnel respond quickly, people already at the scene—staff, faculty, congregants, guards, volunteers, other students—are typically the first to respond. Many times the attack is over before emergency responders arrive.

This fact underscores the need for everyone present to be prepared to act in the safest and most appropriate manner if a situation arises.

Challenges

Targeted attacks on schools and houses of worship are a complex problem, and several factors add to that complexity including:

Vulnerability: Places where people congregate tend to be vulnerable due to:

- Large numbers of potential victims assembled in a limited space. Especially vulnerable are open areas such as corridors and lunchrooms, playgrounds, sanctuaries, student unions, designated areas for fire drills, bus routes, and the like.
- Predictable times when facilities are in use.
- Difficulty preventing an individual from entering or intervening before injuries occur. For example, a metal detector may simply shift the point of attack to an area outside of the venue and may not deter a person bent on harming people.

No crystal ball: Unfortunately there is no easy formula or "profile" of risk factors that accurately determines the next attacker or incident. Profiles are not specific enough to discern who may pose a threat, and they may unfairly stigmatize those who fit some preconceived stereotype. Focusing on stereotypes can also be very misleading: school and campus shooters aren't always students, and attackers at a place of worship may be a member or a stranger.

Competing objectives: Educational and faith-based institutions typically need to balance security against seemingly conflicting objectives, such as:

- Maintaining an open and accessible environment that is conducive to learning and interaction.
- Providing a place of peace and sanctuary where everyone is welcome.

"It can't happen here" mindset: The infrequency of targeted attacks can lead to a sense of security and complacency—an attitude that violence is something that happens only to other people. This perspective sometimes results in resistance to taking preventive measures and reluctance to spend scarce resources on security.

Impact on the community at large: When acts of violence hurt the most vulnerable among us, the impact extends well beyond the walls of the place it occurs. The shock and grief caused by such incidents cause widespread emotional damage and create fear throughout the community. The challenges related to emotional recovery extend to all parts of the community.

Special Challenges

Challenges in Elementary and Secondary Schools:

- **Soft targets** – Schools are inherently soft targets and vulnerable because of many potential targets being concentrated in a limited space. Students are not always in classrooms. Lunchrooms, corridors, outdoor areas, and buses may be difficult to secure.
- **Rural schools** – Many are located in small, isolated towns served by only State police or sheriff's departments. The far-flung patrol responsibilities and limited staff levels of those agencies may result in lengthy response times, and a longer wait for police response extends the period of vulnerability.
- **Vulnerability of information systems** – Information in the first few moments may be scant, fragmentary, and sometimes ambiguous. If administrative personnel (whose offices are often near the main entrance) are killed or driven to take cover, no one may be able to initiate a formal alert, forcing teachers and other staff to make autonomous decisions for the protection of their charges.
- **Young populations** – Young students (especially prekindergarten to grade 3) cannot be counted on to react the same as older students. Young children may not understand instructions. For example, they may not understand the importance of hiding and keeping quiet, or may even hide from responders. The hazard to them and to their teachers is correspondingly greater. This is an especially important consideration for any protocols that involve teaching children to evacuate during an incident.
- **Students with access and functional needs** – Consideration needs to be given to students with access and functional needs before, during, and after an incident.
- **Ineffective approaches to access control** – Many organizations have implemented good access control technologies only to have them compromised by ineffective usage. One example is purchasing a high quality visitor

management system that allows for rapid screening of visitors and then placing the units in a manner where visitors sign themselves in. This usage relies on the integrity of the visitor to maintain security.

- **Employee and student turnover** – Many school systems have turnover rates of up to 25% annually for teaching and support staff. In addition, many schools serve constantly rotating student populations. High rates of turnover can make it more difficult to identify warning behaviors and to keep personnel informed of security protocols.

Challenges in Institutions of Higher Education:

- **Geographical spread** – Colleges often cover large geographic areas, may be geographically integrated in the surrounding community, and sometimes even resemble small towns with the full extent of services in their vicinity (i.e., medical centers, sports complexes, residential centers, businesses). This sprawl complicates security.
- **Access** – Most colleges have open access. Moreover, the population on a campus is so diverse that recognizing an "intruder" can be nearly impossible.
- **Dispersed population** – Autonomy is encouraged and fostered for both students and faculty. At any one time, students, faculty, and staff are dispersed around the campus in classrooms, common areas, cafeterias, offices, dormitories, and numerous other facilities. This arrangement is not conducive to observing and recognizing behavioral concerns among the student population.
- **Lack of regular contact** – The campus population changes from day to day, semester to semester, and year to year. Irregular student schedules minimize regular contact between educators and students, which again makes it more difficult to recognize problem behaviors.
- **Large numbers of international students** – Students who speak English as a second language may find it harder to pick up critical instructions if they are not communicated with great clarity. In addition, many countries do not conduct emergency drills, so students from these countries may be unfamiliar with them.
- **Schedules** – College campuses do not operate under typical business-hour schedules. They are alive and engaged with activity almost around the clock, which magnifies security challenges.
- **Stressors** – Many colleges have residential facilities where students live. The combined educational and residential environment may cause or exacerbate stressors in a student's life and provide triggers for an act of violence by troubled students.
- **Disconnect from students' loved ones** – College students are mostly 18 years old or older—legally adults. Most are living away from home, many for the first time. If faculty and staff observe warning signs in students, they have limited opportunity to interact with parents to discuss their concerns.

Challenges in Houses of Worship:

- **Soft targets** – Many religious leaders are not aware of vulnerabilities and basic crime prevention methods. Consequently, many places of worship are soft targets.
- **Ideology** – By nature houses of worship are open to outsiders and seek to welcome strangers. They may view security measures as inconsistent with this image or fear that they will somehow scare people away. There is a need to balance having a security presence while still keeping the facility open to everyone.
- **Turnover** – Places of worship frequently have a steady turnover of new faces. This, combined with the desire to be welcoming, can make it difficult to identify individuals who are out of place.
- **Predictable schedules** – Houses of worship have predictable hours when people are arriving for worship and then are amassed in a confined area. Some congregations are extremely large ("megachurches" may have as many as 2,000 worshippers a week), providing large numbers of potential targets in one place.
- **Flexible access** – When people gather for worship, things are rarely as organized as they might be in some other meetings. People arrive early and late, in groups and alone. Members and guests may roam around the lobby or wander down halls. The lobby may be packed with people of all ages. If there is more than one service, some people will arrive as others are leaving.
- **Open events** – Places of worship have many events—weddings, receptions, funerals, picnics, community fairs, bazaars, food pantries, self-help group meetings, church camps, and the like—to which nonmembers are invited. These events may be wholly or partly outside and therefore more difficult to secure.
- **Childcare** – Most houses of worship offer childcare, religion classes, camps, and other school-like settings that have the same vulnerabilities as educational institutions.

Everyone Is Part of the Solution

You can't do it alone. Violence is a problem that impacts the entire community, and creating solutions is a joint responsibility involving the whole community. Everyone has an important role to play, including:

- Students and their households.
- School officials, faculty, counselors, staff, and volunteers.
- Religious leaders and congregants.
- Law enforcement, fire service, local emergency managers, and other emergency personnel.
- Judges, mental health professionals, social services, and a variety of other youth-serving professionals.
- Members of the academic and business communities who have expertise to share.

Partners in Preparedness and Planning

Preparedness and planning are the key to making your environment safer. Working together with your community partners will enable you to create a plan that considers:

- Measures you can take **before an incident** to assess and mitigate vulnerabilities.
- Procedures you can use **during an incident** to minimize casualties and help bring the situation under control.
- Actions you can take **after an incident** to promote community recovery.
- What you can do to **stay prepared.**

In later lessons you will learn more about the planning process and ways to prepare in each of these areas.

Quick Reference Guides

The resources below compile key points related to incidents in schools, institutions of higher education, and houses of worship.

Select this link to access a Quick Reference Guide on School Shooters.

Quick Reference Guide: Violence in Houses of Worship

Remember:

- Attacks in houses of worship appear to be rare.
- Many acts of violence are carried out by people with a connection to the congregation.
- The most common violent act at houses of worship is a shooting.
- There are no simple solutions for predicting who will commit violence.
- Acts of violence may be preceded by threats, disputes, or confrontations.

Things To Notice:

Remember, the presence of the following behaviors and appearance do **not** make it likely that someone is going to do harm. However, each has been observed in those who have committed crimes and acts of violence, so it is appropriate to watch for them.

- Sitting in a vehicle for an extended length of time.
- Taking unidentifiable items out of a vehicle.
- Walking or running up to the door and looking around as though on the lookout.

- All threats should be reported to your local law enforcement agency.

Myths:

- That won't happen here.
- That is too minor to report.
- That incident is private.
- Reporting a threat is a wasted effort.
- We don't have *that* type of person here.

Motives:

- Domestic disputes and personal conflicts.
- Robbery.
- Grievances of former members.
- Mental illness.
- Bias against the religion or conflict on specific controversial issues.
- General grievances against society that become associated with the place of worship.

Tips During Worship:

- Be visible.
- Greet members and visitors.
- Report suspicious activity immediately to your local law enforcement agency.

- Walking awkwardly, as though having concealed weapons.
- Two or more unknown people entering together and going different directions.
- Obviously trying to go unnoticed or looking for concealment.
- Displaying unusual emotion (rage, furtiveness, nervousness, fear) or unusual absence of any emotion.
- Standing very still when others are moving forward.
- Doing something that does not fit with the activity at the time, such as standing alone or facing the congregation in the sanctuary instead of sitting.
- Going into areas other than the sanctuary when no one else is present.
- Threatening harm or talking about killing others.
- Wearing unusually inappropriate clothing for a worship environment, especially if bulky enough to conceal weapons.
- Carrying or wearing a bag or backpack, especially if it looks stuffed full.

- Have staff or volunteers monitor general gathering areas and all points of entry.
- Be observant for indicators of unusual emotion, behavior, or appearance that could be linked to problem behavior.

Resources

- U.S. Secret Service, National Threat Assessment Center: http://www.secretservice.gov/ntac.shtml
- National Disaster Interfaiths Network: http://www.n-din.org
- Preparing for Worship Place Violence and Emergencies: http://www.homelandsecurity.ms.gov
- Department of Homeland Security "If You See Something, Say Something" Campaign: http://www.dhs.gov/if-you-see-something-say-something-campaign
- How to Assess the Safety and Security of Your Place of Worship: http://tinalewisrowe.com

Quick Reference Guide: Violence in Institutions of Higher Education (IHEs)

Facts:

- Targeted violence affecting IHEs has increased over the past 20 years.
- Generally as enrollment increases, incidents increase.
- Incidents occur throughout the calendar year.
- The majority of incidents occurred on campus; 20 percent were off campus.
- Most incidents were perpetrated by one individual, who was male.

Tips:

- Plans should equally cover IHE buildings, residences, parking lots, and grounds.
- Campus safety resources should be available year round.
- Have communication between campus safety professionals and municipal law enforcement.
- Establish connections to community resources in advance.
- Have a process for identifying at-risk students.

- The majority of perpetrators were directly affiliated with the institution—current or former student or employee.
- Firearms were used most often, but knives and bladed weapons were used in over 20 percent of the incidents.
- For most incidents the target was one or more specifically named individuals.

Myths:

- Incidents only take place during the school year.
- Only on-campus incidents are relevant.
- Guns are the only concern.
- Attackers frequently travel between buildings.

Motivating Factors:

- Intimate relationship between victim and subject.
- Retaliation for specific action.
- Advances refused or obsession with target.
- Response to academic stress or failure.
- Acquaintance or stranger based sexual violence.
- Psychotic actions.
- Workplace dismissal or sanction.
- Need to kill.
- Draw attention to self or issue.

- Conduct regular security assessments.
- Have campus mental health services available and easily accessible to students.
- Offer specialized mental health services.
- Evaluate writings, drawings, and other individual expression that raise faculty concerns about safety.
- Develop physical and electronic security measures.
- Have a mass notification system and policy.
- Update plans and assessments regularly.
- Form and maintain threat assessment teams.

Threat Assessment Teams

Threat assessment teams seek to evaluate persons of concern by:

- Identifying individuals whose behaviors cause concern or disruption on or off campus.
- Assessing whether the individual has intent and ability to carry out an attack.
- Determining if the individual has taken any preparatory steps for an attack.
- Managing the threat by disrupting it, mitigating the risk, and developing strategies for long-term resolution.

- Bias related.

Resources

- Campus Attacks: Targeted Violence Affecting Institutions of Higher Education: http://www2.ed.gov/admins/lead/safety/campus-attacks.pdf
- Action Guide for Emergency Management at Institutions of Higher Education: http://rems.ed.gov/docs/REMS_ActionGuide.pdf
- Campus Violence Prevention and Response: Best Practices for Massachusetts Higher Education: http://www.mass.edu/library/reports/CampusViolencePreventionAndResponse.pdf

Other Resources

Below are online resources where you can learn more:

- U.S. Secret Service Safe School Initiative
- U.S. Department of Education, Emergency Planning, Office of Safe and Healthy Students
- Centers for Disease Control and Prevention
- National Center for Mental Health Promotion and Youth Violence Prevention
- The Safe Schools/Healthy Students Initiative
- FBI: Campus Attacks: Targeted Violence Affecting Institutions of Higher Education
- U.S. Department of Justice, Bureau of Justice Assistance, Guide for Preventing and Responding to School Violence
- Security Challenges for Houses of Worship

Lesson Summary

You should now be able to identify:

- The threats and challenges associated with mass casualty incidents in schools, institutions of higher education, and houses of worship.
- Lessons learned from past mass casualty incidents.

- The role of the whole community in preventing, protecting, and mitigating against active shooter/mass casualty threats.
- Key factors from incidents where communities were able to prevent an active shooter incident or mitigate mass casualties.

Lesson 2: Getting Started

Getting Started: Establishing a Planning Process

This lesson will describe the steps to take to initiate the process for developing an emergency plan or annex for assault incidents that may result in mass casualties.

At the completion of this lesson, you should be able to identify:

- Key factors in making a partnership-based planning process successful.
- Participants to include in the emergency planning process.
- Elements to include in an emergency plan or annex for mass casualty incidents.
- Resources and guidance available to support the planning process.

Getting Started

Planning for mass casualty incidents is a process based on partnerships. A team approach to planning brings together people who will engage in every aspect of a potential incident—those who seek to prevent, protect against, or mitigate the effects of an incident, those who will become involved if an incident does occur, and those who will help move the community toward recovery.

As partners in planning, team members share expertise that may help prevent an incident or minimize casualties if an incident does occur. And in the process, they build the relationships that will be essential during a coordinated response.

This lesson will help you get started with the planning process, including laying the groundwork for team collaboration, determining functions to be carried out by the team, and identifying resources that can help you complete the planning process.

Introduction

Depending on your situation, the scope of your planning efforts may vary. For example, if you are in a large school district, safety-related policies and plans may be created at the district level, with individual schools focusing their efforts on tailoring the approach to fit their unique situations.

Very small districts, nontraditional and independent schools, places of worship, and college campuses, on the other hand, may be responsible for the entire planning process. If your institution has an existing all-hazards emergency plan, your goal may be to review and update the plan or to create an annex that focuses on active shooter/mass casualty incidents.

Let's begin with some basic guidelines that will help you establish an effective planning process.

Planning Guidelines

Five simple guidelines can enhance your planning for a safer, more secure environment.

1. Partnerships: Lay a foundation of partnerships.
2. Process: Commit to the process.
3. People: Involve the right people.
4. Pacing: Pace yourself for success.
5. Plans: Customize your plan.

Laying a Foundation of Partnerships

Planning begins by creating partnerships. A team effort requires coordination among many individuals and organizations with diverse expertise and perspectives.

Throughout the planning process, participants become more aware of the challenges, learn about the contributions of all partners, and gain a more indepth understanding of procedures and protocols.

A partnership approach to planning fosters a whole community commitment to enhancing safety and security.

Benefits of Partnerships

A partnership approach to planning:

- Enhances awareness of key issues and protective measures.
- Helps ensure that procedures are realistic and comprehensive.
- Fosters community buy-in and ownership.
- Creates shared responsibility among partners.
- Brings creativity and innovation to your planning efforts.
- Prevents resistance to and misunderstanding of the measures.
- Provides reassurance that safety and security are important.
- Ensures specific community needs are addressed.
- Helps in the understanding and acceptance of roles.

- Aids in familiarity of the site and procedures by all partners.
- Helps to ensure that the plans for your institution are compatible with those of the agencies that would respond if an incident occurred.

Laying a Foundation of Partnerships – Example

Waukegan Public Schools in Illinois developed some of the most comprehensive school crisis plans in their state. The plans include:

- Role-specific emergency charts for the superintendent, administrators, teachers, custodians, school secretaries, food service personnel, and school bus drivers and an after-hours event chart.
- A series of customized training videos that show students and staff how to implement protocols such as lockdown and reverse evacuation.
- A variety of short web courses and training sessions for staff.
- A robust approach to drills that requires various staff to implement emergency protocols when prompted by a scenario presented by an administrator each month.

The plans were developed with assistance from a wide variety of area public safety agencies, administrators, teachers, and support staff and have been tested by a progressive exercise program including school level drills, tabletop exercises, functional exercises, and a full-scale exercise that were externally evaluated.

Committing to the Process

The process of creating the plan—forging partnerships, gaining insight into each other's perspectives, communicating, and working together—leads to the ability to function as a team during a crisis.

Committing full effort to the process of planning will prepare you to handle situations together when they arise.

Involving the Right People

Third, involve the right people. We'll come back to this in more detail, but the main ideas are these:

- **Anyone who will be involved in implementing the plan should be involved in creating it.** Plans should not be developed in a vacuum. Relationships need to be built in advance so that emergency responders and others are familiar with your organization.
- **Don't overlook expertise within your organization or constituency.** For example, who knows your facility better than your own building maintenance or custodial crew?

Involving the Right People: Examples

- Who safeguards the youth when traveling to and from your site? Bus or van drivers, crossing guards.
- Who is likely to answer a bomb threat call? Office staff or volunteers.
- Who is present when people are gathered for meals? Cafeteria staff and volunteers.
- Who has first contact with visitors at a place of worship? Greeters.

There likely is plenty of talent among your staff, volunteers, congregation, or parent organization who can contribute ideas. Faith-based organizations, for example, usually represent a cross-section of the community, with all its skills and knowledge. The same is true of parent groups. Find out how they can help you!

Pacing Yourself for Success

Next, consider the pace of your planning process. A common planning pitfall is trying to move too quickly to the end stage.

First, don't be in too great a hurry to produce an end product. Set a realistic timetable, and pace the work so there is adequate time for information gathering, assessment, consideration of alternatives, exchange of ideas, and thorough analysis.

Second, pace the development of your capabilities. It will be important to practice putting the plan into action, but this is best done incrementally. For example, an exercise that involves combinations of response actions and multiple agencies is likely to fail if attempted too early. Plan to practice individual actions or functions, such as communications, lockdown, or reverse evacuation procedures, and build gradually toward more complex exercises.

Customizing Your Plan

Finally, remember that plans aren't one-size-fits-all. Just as no two schools, campuses, or places of worship are alike, their plans shouldn't be identical. Avoid purchasing a ready-made plan or simply copying the plan of another organization. Other plans can serve as useful models, but what may work in one place may not work in another.

Invest the effort to develop your own plan—one that's right for your facility and your organization. Although more initial effort is required, the long-term benefits are significant.

That is not to say you can't learn from other organizations like yours—far from it. Talk to them, find out what they learned in the planning process, and consider how to use those lessons to enhance your own planning.

Tips for Customizing Your Plan

- Plans that are not reflective of local risks, realities, and resources are not only more prone to failure in a crisis. They can be difficult to defend in a court of law if litigation occurs in the wake of an incident.
- Plan development is another opportunity for input from emergency management and from local law enforcement, fire service, and other first responders.
- Response capabilities and approaches used by public safety responders vary widely across the nation. The most effective plans recognize and reflect these realities.
- Remember that preparing employees and volunteers to recognize danger, take immediate life-saving action, and communicate the danger to others is one of best opportunities we have to minimize the loss of life in a mass casualty incident.

Functions of the Planning Team

Planning is a continuous process, and partners in that process may perform many different functions along the way, including:

- Gathering and analyzing information.
- Conducting vulnerability assessments.
- Developing measures and plans to address vulnerabilities.
- Identifying potential resources to support planning efforts.
- Helping to train personnel and exercise the plans.
- Identifying lessons learned and updating plans.

You will want to identify potential planning team members who can help perform these functions.

Who Should Be on the Planning Team?

Start identifying partners by looking inside your organization.

Consider the following:

- Administrators and leaders.
- Staff and volunteers.
- Parents/guardians, congregants, and students.
- Advocates for those with access and functional needs.
- Internal law enforcement such as campus police or security personnel.

Consider individuals who are respected and trusted. Also consider those individuals who have knowledge or expertise in an important area.

Selecting Team Members From Within

Select team members who are:

- Familiar with the organization and the setting.
- Knowledgeable about what is desired for safety, security, and preparedness.
- Effective and open communicators.
- Balanced in approach and not excessive about any one aspect of the process.
- Able to do the tasks required and to schedule the time needed.

Administrators and Leaders

Identify administrators and leaders in your organization who have:

- Decisionmaking authority.
- An understanding of the planning goals.
- Ability to advocate for resources.

Unofficial leaders—those who are trusted and looked to for leadership—can be especially helpful in engaging the interest and assistance of others in the organization.

Staff and Volunteers

Identify staff members and volunteers who can contribute. Examples include faculty, faith-based leaders, counselors, office staff, maintenance and other support staff, security personnel, student housing supervisors, transportation, staff that handle money, and ushers and greeters. Look for people who have:

- Trusted relationships within and outside the organization. Such relationships can enable them to recognize threat indicators, concerns within the community, and possible resistance or other obstacles to planning.
- Expertise in a specific area, such as:
- First aid and triage.
- Counseling.
- Working with persons with access and functional needs.
- Speaking the languages of the community.
- Technology, information technology, or security.
- Facility maintenance.
- Transportation.
- Campus housing.
- Handling and safe-keeping of money.
- Responsibilities for recognizing members and interacting with visitors.
- Knowledge of onsite and offsite activities/events, of schedules, and of those who have access to keys, codes, etc.

Parents/guardians, congregants, and students

Identify people in the extended "family" (e.g., PTA and congregation members) who have:

- Special expertise related to their field of work that might pertain to protection, mitigation, response, or recovery from violent incidents (e.g., law enforcement, mental health, medical services, security, insurance, public information and media relations).
- Trusted relationships with the community that would be helpful for engaging community support.

Students and Other Children

Identify students or children in your care who are trusted by their peers. Students can often:

- Provide insight different from that of adults.
- Alert school officials to problems that have gone undetected.
- Help build support among peers for measures or programs.
- Assist in establishing a security culture among their peers.
- Participate in peer mediation, teen courts, and other problem-solving programs.

Next, identify potential community partners who will be part of the response or whose expertise can add to the process. CPG 101, Developing and Maintaining Emergency Operations Plans, recommends including the following partners on your team. You may wish to tailor your team to the specific needs of your organization.

- Emergency management
- Agriculture

- Law enforcement
- Fire services
- EMS
- Public health
- Hospitals and health care facilities
- Public works
- Utility operators
- Education
- Animal control
- Social services
- Childcare, child welfare, and juvenile justice facilities (including courts)
- National Guard
- Private sector
- Civic, social, faith-based, educational, professional, and advocacy organizations

Examples of Team Collaboration

Team Participants	Examples
Emergency management	Emergency management agencies provide support to schools, houses of worship, and institutions of higher education through resources. Some examples are: • Foundations for Preparedness Collin County, TX: http://www.co.collin.tx.us/preparedness/index.jsp#foundations • Virginia Department of Emergency Management: http://www.vaemergency.gov/em-community/plans/eop-templates-college • Georgia Emergency Management Agency/Homeland Security: http://www.gema.ga.gov **Source:** http://www.campussafetymagazine.com/Channel/Emergency-Management/articles/2009/09/Emergency-Managers-Can-Be-Invaluable-Resources.aspx
Law enforcement	The relationship that one university built with local law enforcement helped stop a former employee from obtaining a weapons permit in a neighboring jurisdiction. **Source:** http://www.securitymanagement.com/article/teaming-reduce-risk
Fire services	A school district safety coordinator collaborated with local fire departments to help train classroom teachers. "They helped us with the training, provided us facilities, and let us use their resources and expertise." **Source:** http://rems.ed.gov/docs/SS_Vol01Issue01_LincolnCounty.pdf Fire service personnel are often very good at helping to figure out how to move large groups of people quickly and to resolve issues such as whether or not you can tell people to ignore the fire alarm in a lockdown situation.

Healthcare	In Florida, a hospital trained representatives from houses of worship on spiritual care, stress care, and how to provide care for a loved one. **Source:** http://www.emergencymgmt.com/disaster/Florida-County-Faith-Based-Community.html One university included a liaison from the local hospital as part of its response to mass casualties. The liaison will coordinate communications with medical personnel to ensure they are prepared in the case of mass casualties. **Source:** http://www.campussafetymagazine.com/Channel/University-Security/articles/2011/05/Community-Partnerships-Improve-Active-Shooter-Response.aspx
Mental health	After the suicide of a student, the Critical Incident Stress Management (CISM) team was brought in to help the personnel deal with the incident. From that incident, a partnership was formed in which school counselors received training and participated on the team. **Source:** http://www.greenfieldreporter.com/view/local_story/ NPHS_struggles_to_cope_with_lo_1336095551 A university representative described the importance of coming together as a collective team and to weigh different pieces of information from different perspectives, including that of a psychologist and university counsel. **Source:** http://www.npr.org/templates/story/story.php?storyId=124007555
Private Sector	A bakery in Vermont used social media to articulate community needs and partnered with the interfaith council to assist the needs of the community. Ultimately, through the long-term recovery, this relationship was important in focusing on the needs of survivors. **Source:** http://www.fema.gov/blog/2012-08-24/faith-based-community-organizations-whole-community-approach-emergency-management A school district's partnership with local businesses created a synergy that led to local businesses printing calendars with safety messages, insurance companies helping to sponsor community safety expositions, and suppliers discounting safety equipment and providing funding for the district's Teen CERT (Community Emergency Response Team) program. **Source:** http://rems.ed.gov/docs/TapIn2CmunityPartnrs4ERMgmt.pdf

| **Community and volunteer organizations** | A community college included the American Heart Association as a part of their emergency management team. This relationship came in handy when they had to address the need to train people on automatic external defibrillators (AEDs) and CPR.
Source:
http://rems.ed.gov/docs/SS_Vol01Issue03_DaytonaState.pdf

When eight secretaries from area houses of worship requested assistance on how to handle the ever-growing issues of financial requests, representatives from nonprofit agencies, a university, and area house of worship leaders developed a group that was able to assist with community needs and restore a sense of safety with personnel in the houses of worship.
Source:
http://collaboration.foundationcenter.org/search/narratives.php?id=4225 |
| **District and peer organizations** | A school district planned to provide special training sessions and emergency identification to members of the faith community who agreed to respond and provide assistance at the family reunification center in the event of a crisis.
Source: Dorn, M., Thomas. G., Wong, M., & Shepherd, S. (2004). *Jane's Safe Schools Planning Guide for All Hazards, first edition.* Surrey, UK: Jane's Information Group.

Montana Safe Schools Center at the University of Montana provides resources and training to schools.
Source:
http://iers.umt.edu/Montana_Safe_Schools_Center/default.php |

Conducting Planning Meetings

Everyone on a planning team has other responsibilities. To ensure their continued support and participation, it is important to respect their time and ensure that the meetings are efficient and productive. The following approaches can help keep meetings on track:

- Manage the time: Identify, and stick to, a specific start and end time for meetings.
- Provide a clear agenda with meeting items prioritized.
- Assign a meeting facilitator.
- Take and distribute meeting minutes.
- Identify action items for subsequent meetings.

Follow through on unfinished business.

Meeting Tips

Tip	Explanation
Clarify the meeting goals	Identify the goals of the meeting and document the outcomes that you think would come from an effective meeting.
Have a written agenda	Develop a written agenda as a roadmap to achieving the meeting goals. Circulate the agenda before the meeting and, if appropriate, invite attendees to add items to it. During the meeting, use the agenda to provide structure and stay on track.
Set enough time	A common mistake that leaders and facilitators make is to try to get done more than what is achievable within a given timeframe. Don't make this mistake. If you want the meeting to be effective, then it is worth giving the right amount of time to it.
Start on time	Start the meeting on time whether everyone is there or not. Doing so sets an example of efficiency and sends the message that you value the team members' time. It also encourages latecomers to be on time for the next meeting.
Assign a facilitator	A facilitator keeps the meeting on track and moving forward and helps ensure that all participants have the opportunity to be heard.
Appoint a recorder	The recorder's role is to take notes during the meeting and distribute minutes afterward. Minutes keep everyone on the same page and provide an opportunity to clarify any misunderstandings before moving on to next steps.
Provide an orientation	Stating the purpose of the meeting at the outset takes very little time but will mean that everybody is on the same wavelength. Providing an orientation becomes especially important as the group evolves.
Hear team members' interests	An effective way to start a series of meetings is to quickly hear from each member about their interest in being at the meeting. Set a time limit (e.g., 1 minute per person) and stick to it. Invite people to be open about their reason for attending.
Agree on ground rules	A simple list of ground rules—such as asking people to turn off their cell phones, limit side conversations,

	listen and then only add new ideas, and speak respectfully—can make a huge difference in the tone and feeling of the meeting. Additional ground rules relate to aspects of how the group operates, such as: - Roles of team members. - Confidentiality. - Openness. - Communication processes. - Commitment of resources. - Commitment to results.
Regularly get input from everyone involved	When appropriate, quickly go around the room and give each person the opportunity to say how they see the situation. Again, set a time limit (e.g., 2-3 minutes each) and strictly stick to the time limit. This approach is simple, effective, keeps everyone (including those who seldom speak up) involved, and takes little time.
Find common ground	A group is more likely to take action to effect change when they have come to some agreement as to the desired future. This usually takes the form of agreement around the strategic areas that require focusing on in order to achieve the purpose.
Action planning	The last step of any meeting should be devoted to action planning—who is going to do what by when to achieve the identified objectives. Take the final minutes of the meeting to restate the commitments that people have made.
Action from previous meeting	If the meeting is part of a regular series of meetings, recount each of the action plans that were agreed on at the previous meeting and have the responsible individuals indicate what progress they have made on it. (This makes it clear that people will be held accountable.)
Improve future meetings	Ask team members how you can improve future meetings. The best way to do this without it becoming a gripe session is to first ask, "What has worked well in our meetings in the past?" Once the group has explored that, then ask, "What can we do to make our meetings even more effective?"

End on time	Again this sends a message of respect to the attendees. The one exception to this rule is if **all** team members agree to extend the finish time.

Gathering Critical Information and Resources

Planning begins by gathering and reviewing existing information. We have talked about the types of expertise team members can bring to the process. Critical information for the planning process can also be gathered with their help. Important information includes:

- Historical information.
- Related plans, policies, procedures, and legal requirements.
- Demographic and logistical information.
- Information about current security and safety measures.
- Safety-related concerns of students, staff, or congregants (e.g., from climate surveys).

Checklist for Information Gathering

- ☐ Historical information:
    - o ☐ Past incidents.
    - o ☐ Threat assessments, including those from Federal, State, and local law enforcement.
    - o ☐ Information on school culture and climate.
- ☐ Related plans, policies, and procedures:
    - o ☐ Existing community-based plans.
    - o ☐ Emergency response policies and procedures provided by your district or governing body.
    - o ☐ Existing plans for your facility, such as all-hazards emergency plan, continuity of operations plan, etc.
    - o ☐ Relevant regulations, ordinances, guidelines, and legal requirements that pertain to protection, mitigation, response, and recovery.
    - o ☐ Agreements between your organization and other organizations.
    - o ☐ Other documents recommended by your team.
- ☐ Demographic information:
    - o ☐ Typical numbers of people within facilities, including:
        - ▪ ☐ Student population and attendance.
        - ▪ ☐ Faculty, staff, and volunteers.

- ▪ ☐ Average numbers of worshippers per service.
        - ▪ ☐ Children in childcare.
        - ▪ ☐ Attendance at special events.
    - ○ ☐ Organization charts, member lists, and contact information.
    - ○ ☐ Information about vendors, consultants, service companies, and others who enter the premises.
  - • ☐ Logistical information:
    - ○ ☐ Site surveys that contain:
        - ▪ ☐ Building floor plans including blueprints or drawings, maps that identify the location of hazardous materials, elevators, and entrances.
        - ▪ ☐ Plans of utility, communications, and alarm systems that identify/map leads for water, gas, electricity, cable, telephones, and HVAC.
        - ▪ ☐ Grounds plans including drawings of fences, maps, and buildings.
    - ○ ☐ Transportation information (e.g., bus schedules, traffic controls, and parking procedures).
    - ○ ☐ Schedules, including regular operations planned activities, events, and holidays.
    - ○ ☐ Identities of personnel who have master keys, codes, and access to secured areas.
    - ○ ☐ Supplies: Emergency kits, available emergency medical supplies.
  - • ☐ Current security and safety measures, such as:
    - ○ ☐ Access control systems.
    - ○ ☐ Surveillance and monitoring systems.
    - ○ ☐ Arrangements with law enforcement for patrols.
    - ○ ☐ Agreements with neighboring properties.
    - ○ ☐ Visitor screening procedures.
  - • ☐ Other relevant information, such as:
    - ○ ☐ Current trends.
    - ○ ☐ Climate surveys.

Aligning With Other Plans

Mass casualty response planning is part of an all-hazards approach to planning, and the procedures you develop for addressing acts of aggression and mass casualty incidents will become part of your comprehensive all-hazards emergency plan.

It is also important that your planning efforts for such incidents be aligned with other plans. Through the planning process, team members should review and maintain linkages to all related plans, including:

Individual and family emergency plans: Household members may not be together when an incident occurs, so it is important to have plans for getting to a safe place, contacting one another, and reuniting. Ensuring personnel have plans to ensure the safety of their loved ones helps them focus on the needs of the organization when an incident occurs.

Facility emergency/crisis plans: Your facility's emergency or crisis plan is an ongoing plan for responding to a wide variety of potential hazards. It describes how people and property will be protected; details who is responsible for carrying out specific actions; identifies the personnel, equipment, facilities, supplies, and other resources available; and outlines how all actions will be coordinated.

Your facility's emergency or crisis plan also identifies the use of the organization's facilities in emergency situations, such as using it for a shelter, reception area, staging area, point of emergency supply and food distribution, or alternate government facility. Organizations need this information so they can address the issues in their planning.

Community and State Emergency Operations Plans: Emergency operations plans for the community or State are ongoing plans for responding to a wide variety of potential hazards. The emergency or crisis plans for your facility should be developed and exercised in close collaboration with local or community plans. Community plans in turn should be developed and exercised in conjunction with State and regional plans. At the State level, emergency plans should be designed to respond to citizens' needs and to outline when to turn to the Federal Government for assistance.

Continuity Plans: Continuity plans outline essential functions that must be performed during an incident that disrupts normal operations and how these functions will be performed. They also describe the process for resuming normal operations following an emergency.

Outlining Your Planning Documents

If you already have a comprehensive emergency operations plan, then your team may be updating that plan or adding an annex. Hazard/threat-specific annexes typically include information on:

- Vulnerability assessment.
- Actions to mitigate the threat.
- Protective actions.
- Internal and external communication procedures.

- Response and short-term stabilization actions.
- Recovery actions.

General Tips for Planning

- Identify where you are vulnerable. (The next lesson will provide information about assessing and mitigating vulnerabilities.)
- Be sure the plan is based on fact, not assumptions.
- Consider incidents before, during, and after typical operating hours.
- Include offsite events, such as stadium events, field trips, and camps.
- Be comprehensive and redundant. Don't overly rely on a single approach. Identify backup personnel for key roles.
- Base the plan on current information, and keep it current. If your building layout changes, update it in the plan. Update contact information regularly.
- Be sure your plan is age appropriate. There are significant differences in how elementary school children, high school students, college students, and members of a congregation will behave in a crisis.
- Be aware of the diverse needs of individuals, including those with access and functional needs or limited English proficiency.
- Consider how you will communicate with staff, volunteers, students, community members, and the media during and after a crisis.
- Consider what training will be needed to make the plan effective.
- Use a plan format that is clear and easy to use.
- Include timelines, milestones, and responsibilities for completing them.

Creating the Plan

Guidance is available to help you create a plan. For example, Comprehensive Preparedness Guide (CPG) 101, Developing and Maintaining Emergency Operations Plans, provides detailed information on:

- Steps in the planning process.
- What information to include in a plan or annex.
- Obtaining input, review, and approval.
- Disseminating, implementing, and maintaining a plan.

In addition, your local emergency manager may be able to assist with planning, and several courses on plan development are available from FEMA.

Planning Resources

- CPG 101, Developing and Maintaining Emergency Operations Plans, provides Federal Emergency Management Agency (FEMA) guidance on the fundamentals of planning and developing emergency operations plans (EOPs). CPG 101 shows that EOPs are connected to planning efforts in the areas of prevention, protection, response, recovery, and mitigation.

Training:

- IS-36: Multi-Hazard Planning for Childcare
- IS-235: Emergency Planning
- E/L103: Planning: Emergency Operations
- E/L361: Multi-Hazard Emergency Planning for Schools
- L363: Multi-Hazard Emergency Planning for Higher Education

Resources and Guidance

You can use the following resources to learn more about building teams and developing plans. Although organized according to venue, each contains ideas that are useful in any environment.

General:

- Collaboration: Key to a Successful Partnership. Presents simple guidelines for collaboration.

Schools:

- FEMA course IS-362, Multihazard Emergency Planning for Schools. Covers basic information about developing, implementing, and maintaining a school emergency operations plan (EOP).
- Practical Information on Crisis Planning: A Guide for Schools and Communities. Presents critical concepts and components of good crisis planning, stimulates thinking about the crisis preparedness process, and provides examples of promising practices.
- Steps for Developing a School Emergency Plan. Includes helpful hints for school planning.
- Components of Comprehensive School & District Emergency Management Plans. Provides a checklist of items to be included.

Institutions of Higher Education:

- Action Guide for Emergency Management at Institutions of Higher Education. Serves as a resource for developing and implementing an emergency management plan at a higher education institution.

Houses of Worship:

- <u>Checklist for a Church Emergency Management Plan</u>. Provides a guide for the leadership of a faith-based organization to evaluate its readiness to respond to an emergency.
- <u>Be a Ready Congregation: Tip Sheets for U.S. Religious Leaders</u>. Provides tip sheets by the National Disaster Interfaiths Network, including Active Shooter in a House of Worship and others.

Lesson Summary

You should now understand the importance of creating partnerships to plan for a secure and safe environment, and how these partnerships help you develop a plan by providing expertise and resources.

Subsequent lessons will discuss specific aspects of the environment that should be considered before, during, and after an incident.

Lesson 3: Before an Incident

Before an Incident: Assessing and Mitigating Vulnerabilities

This lesson will describe the process for assessing security measures and mitigating vulnerabilities that are identified.

After completing this lesson, you should be able to identify:

- Key considerations in conducting a security assessment.
- The role of individuals in mitigating vulnerabilities.
- Characteristics of an effective safety and security program.

Introduction

Preparedness is an ongoing process. Being prepared helps to lessen the likelihood of an incident occurring by reducing vulnerabilities. Preparedness can also reduce the negative consequences should an incident occur. Making your school or place of worship a safer place requires bringing together your institution's internal resources and those of the community to identify and mitigate vulnerabilities.

Efforts to reduce your vulnerability to mass casualty incidents will be more effective if they are based on a comprehensive security assessment. An effective security program addresses three main areas:

- Identifying any physical or situational aspects of the facility that increase your vulnerability.
- Engaging people as active participants in maintaining a secure and safe environment.
- Initiating measures for addressing vulnerabilities that have been identified.

Preparedness

As described in Presidential Policy Directive 8, National Preparedness, and the National Preparedness Goal, preparedness encompasses a wide range of activities in the following areas:

- **Prevention:** Prevent, avoid or stop an imminent, threatened or actual act of terrorism.

- **Protection:** Protect our citizens, residents, visitors, and assets against the greatest threats and hazards in a manner that allows our interests, aspirations, and way of life to thrive.
- **Mitigation:** Reduce the loss of life and property by lessening the impact of future disasters.
- **Response:** Respond quickly to save lives, protect property and the environment, and meet basic human needs in the aftermath of a catastrophic incident.
- **Recovery:** Recover through a focus on the timely restoration, strengthening and revitalization of infrastructure, housing and a sustainable economy, as well as the health, social, cultural, historic and environmental fabric of communities affected by a catastrophic incident.

Notice that efforts to avoid or avert an incident (other than terrorism) fall within the area of protection. Together, protection and mitigation measures can lessen the chances of an incident happening and reduce the negative impacts if one does occur.

Assessing Vulnerabilities

Preparedness for mass casualty incidents requires a combination of physical, technological, and environmental security strategies as well as proactive policies and procedures.

In making your organization a safer place, a good first step is to conduct a security assessment.

Conducting an assessment involves taking a close, systematic look at a variety of things that could affect security, including physical, situational, and procedural factors.

It means walking the neighborhood and grounds, conducting online research, and interacting with local law enforcement to become better informed about community crime risks.

It means inspecting the physical facility, systems, and equipment; reviewing policies and procedures; talking to people; thinking about human interactions and situational factors; and asking yourselves "What if…?"

Security assessments are not a one-time event. Keeping them up to date requires an ongoing process and a safety mindset—maintaining a level of awareness and asking, Are we doing what is needed to keep this place safe and secure?

Security Assessment

A security assessment:

- Is an ongoing process for identifying and evaluating potential risks and areas of weakness that could have adverse consequences.
- Provides a basis for planning and implementing protective and mitigation measures.
- Looks at more than the physical environment. An effective assessment reviews the overall climate for security and safety, including policies, procedures, resources, training, and exercises.

Site Surveys

Site surveys should be completed in each facility every year. Similarly, annual surveys of staff, students, volunteers, and/or members are one of the most reliable ways to identify risk before someone gets hurt.

The site survey is a complete inspection of the facility and grounds to make sure every relevant feature of the building is recorded. Items that can be important to those who respond in an emergency include:

- Schematic plans for the building.
- Location of power main and all electrical panels.
- Location of controls and operating instructions for emergency systems such as fire alarms and sprinkler systems.
- Location of telephone boxes.
- Phone and address listings for all critical personnel.
- Emergency phone listings for all possible emergency responders, maintenance personnel, and key system officials.
- Locations for assembly of evacuated personnel, suitable emergency command center spots, and rescue helicopter landing sites.
- Location and routes to nearby emergency medical facilities.
- Location of emergency contact records.

The results of a site survey are recorded in written form, and copies are placed in secure storage at the site and at various public safety facilities. This ensures the information can be retrieved quickly no matter where the crisis takes place or how widespread it may be.

Remember to look at environmental factors. It is very important to view security in relation to the unique nature of the environment being assessed.

For example, in K-12 schools and faith-based organizations with youth programs, evaluating student supervision is an important security consideration. Effective student supervision can reduce the risk of serious injury and death from almost any threat. Improving supervision can reduce the impact of bullying, gang activity, dangerous medical emergencies, and natural hazards, as well as incidents like weapons assaults which are often linked to poor student supervision. Many school weapons assaults occur during fights which can often be prevented with good student supervision. In addition, people who are being properly supervised can be more quickly secured or evacuated from danger.

Why Conduct a Security Assessment?

Historically, site weaknesses have made it easier for incidents to occur and harder for personnel to intervene quickly. For example, at some incident sites:

- Offenders had easy access into the facility.
- Occupants had inadequate escape paths.
- Staff or volunteers were unable to spot threats in time.
- Staff were not trained and empowered to take independent life-saving actions under the extreme stress of an actual incident.
- Communication was inadequate.

A security assessment often identifies site vulnerabilities. The assessment process provides an opportunity to work with community partners to identify, correct, and prevent problems. It also fosters communication with those that would be involved in a crisis situation.

Assessment Process Overview

A security assessment includes:

- Reviewing past incidents, threat assessments, and existing policy and procedures.
- Considering how risk factors in your own organization and in the surrounding community impact your security.
- Walking through the facility to identify physical vulnerabilities.
- Interviewing key personnel to assess effectiveness of procedures.
- Identifying existing resources and capabilities that can be used to address a vulnerability.
- Reporting the findings, including positive observations, vulnerabilities, and recommended corrective actions.

When planning the assessment, it is helpful to think in terms of layers of security.

Layers of Security

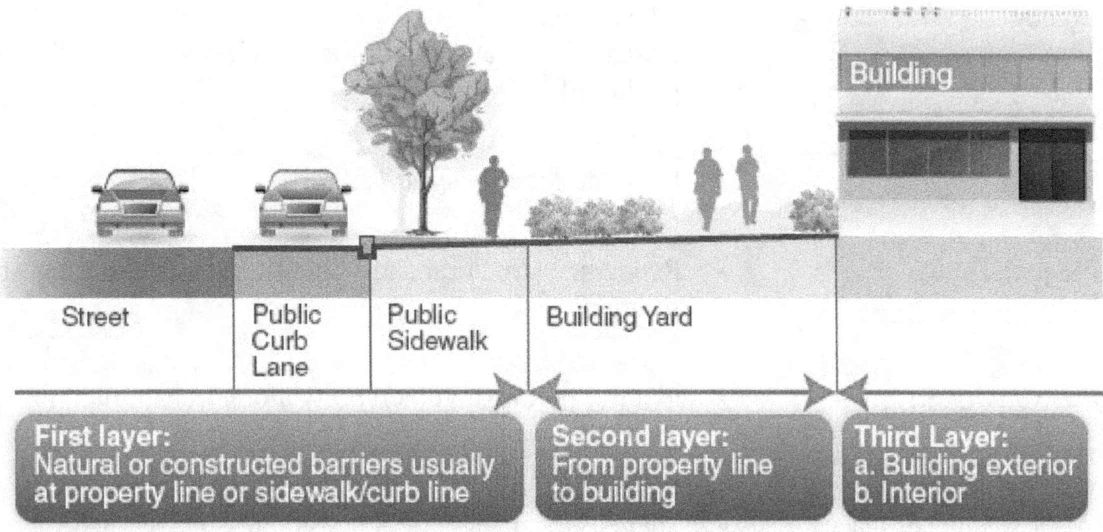

Forming an Assessment Team

Using a team approach brings a variety of perspectives to the assessment process. In forming your assessment team, begin with members of your planning team and call on others, as needed, for specific expertise. Below are examples of how particular team members can help:

Team Members	How They Can Help
Law enforcement	• Provide information on neighborhood crime patterns and history. • Assist with the facility walk-through.
School resource officer or other security personnel	• Contribute firsthand knowledge of existing vulnerabilities and experience in responding to incidents.
Fire department	• Evaluate fire safety. • Assist with evaluating changes in security that can conflict with fire codes such as locking systems. • Assist in identifying means of attack using fire or chemicals.

Emergency management or homeland security agency	<ul><li>Provide information on community profile, past incidents, resource acquisition, and incident management.</li><li>Assist with balancing conflicting viewpoints of other public safety disciplines.</li></ul>
Security company	• Evaluate security systems.
Custodial staff	• Recognize structural and property hazards and suggest solutions.
Bus/van drivers	• Identify points of vulnerability along transportation routes.
Other schools or places of worship	• Share assessment experience and lessons learned.

Tips for Assessment Team Success

- **Share tasks to avoid overloading a few people.**
- **Schedule several assessing sessions.** Two to four hours seems to be the time span that is most effective for volunteer teams.
- **Designate a leader or co-leaders** to coordinate, schedule, lead the way during the assessment, and make sure the paperwork is done.
- **Keep each team small.** Consider breaking up a larger team into smaller ones (ideally three or four people) and start at opposite ends of an area.
- **Avoid assessment team pitfalls.** Common problems include:
  - Some people hurrying too much and others moving too slowly.
  - Being excessive or unreasonable either about concerns or solutions.
  - Losing interest and not participating.
  - Focusing on being the first to find problems, rather than on helping the team assess both weaknesses and strengths.
  - Considering assessment findings as criticisms of self or others.
- **Take action about what is observed in the assessment.** If it is serious, act immediately.

— Adapted from Tina Lewis Rowe (www.tinalewisrowe.com)

Identifying Situational Risk Factors

As part of your assessment, consider situational factors that create or add to risk for your facility. Doing this at the outset may help focus your attention on related physical vulnerabilities during the walk-through.

Examples:

- Does your place of worship have valuable assets (money from offerings, valuable artifacts) onsite that could invite break-ins? Are emotion-laden activities (e.g., divorce workshops or domestic abuse counseling) conducted? Is there a public connection with controversial issues?
- Is your school or campus affected by a culture and climate that includes gang hostility, drug activity, alcohol abuse, or aggressive environments?
- Does the layout of your facility (e.g., sprawling, or integrated into an urban environment) make it difficult to control access?

Assessment Tips

Tip: Before or during the assessment, try brainstorming "what-if" scenarios (what/where/when) as a focus for evaluating security. For example: What if someone stashed a weapon on an outside window sill to avoid detection when entering the building, intending to retrieve it from inside? Or, what if someone brought a concealed weapon to a worship service intending to settle a grievance?

Scenarios can help focus your attention on useful questions such as:

- What might happen in this space?
- What might prevent it from happening?
- What actions might reduce the harm?
- What kind of communications would we need?
- What plans and procedures do we need for handling this situation?
- How would persons in this area secure themselves from an armed aggressor?
- How would staff or trained volunteers communicate danger and instruct people to quickly enact protective actions?

Getting Ready for the Walk-Through

Before conducting a walk through:

- Make a plan and a schedule.

- Gather all the supplies you will need for the assessment.
- If a prior site survey is not available, create your own maps to organize the inspection:
    - Plot outside areas. Walk off the dimensions and include boundaries, streets, walkways, parking areas, playgrounds, landscaping areas, and other features.
    - Diagram the building with a separate graph for each floor. Mark doors and windows, and include rooms, open spaces, passageways, and other security-related features.

Assessment Supply Checklist

Supplies	Description
Flashlight	One for each team member.
Screwdriver	A tool with a tip or point.
Paper and pen	A three-ring binder with paper or survey forms is better than a clipboard or a legal pad because it allows you to flip back and forth through pages as needed.
Digital camera	A camera for taking basic close-up photos. Have a fully charged battery with a spare. A camera with an optical viewfinder (not only an LCD screen) allows easier viewing in a variety of light conditions.
Keys and codes	You will need to be able to open up every door and space, unless it is a private office space. Have all the keys or codes, or a master key or code, or have a maintenance person available to unlock doors. Key control is a process that needs to be assessed as well.
Emergency plan or procedures	Any directions, advice, or suggestions provided to users of the space should be checked during the assessment to see if they appear to be valid and appropriate.
Cell phone and a list of contact numbers	Have a way to contact facility staff in case there is need for notification or questions during the assessment.
Binoculars	Binoculars can be very helpful in inspecting things from a distance, such as checking a security camera that is mounted high on a rooftop.
Laser rangefinder	Laser rangefinders can be used to quickly measure distance such as an evacuation site for an explosives-related incident.
Moist hand wipes	Doing a thorough assessing can be dusty or dirty work.

Organizing the Walk-Through

It is important to develop a systematic approach so that nothing is missed during assessment. One approach is to use the layers of security.

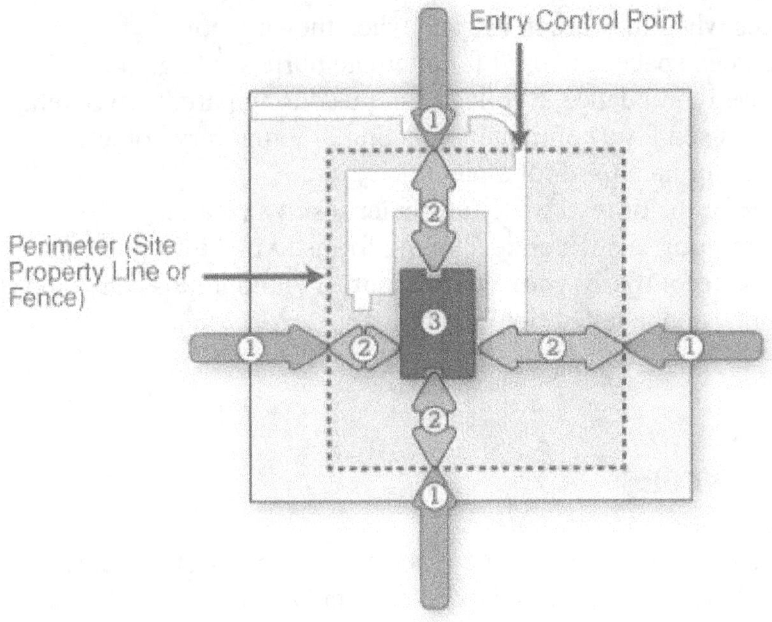

A Standard Approach

Use a standard approach for assessing each area. In each space, stand or sit and thoroughly observe the area, considering it from the viewpoints of both people who will be using the space and a person who intends harm. Make notes about potentially problematic conditions you observe.

- How is the space typically used, and by whom? Are there other uses to consider?
- Does some aspect of the space increase the risk or worsen the consequences?
- Are there protective aspects of the space that should be noted?
- What actions could correct or reduce a problem?
- What emergency procedures are needed?

Before leaving an area, do one more walk-through. Do not rush, even in familiar areas.

Approach Tips

- **Be thorough.** Practice focused observation and purposeful inspection, and allow enough time to be thorough.
- **Be flexible in your approach.** Consider how conducting the inspection in different ways can give better results. For example:
  - Include inspections on different days of the week and times (including evenings).
  - Look at spaces when they are in use and when they are not.
  - Think about when spaces are used for alternate purposes (e.g., a gymnasium used for a dance, a college campus during parents' weekend, a religious space used for a community meeting or temporary homeless shelter, an outdoor area used for a picnic).
- **Take useful notes.** Take the time to write full sentences in a clear, orderly manner for ease of reporting. Consider developing forms to make the job easier.
- **Take photographs to accompany your written notes.** Photographs can help you prepare a more accurate and detailed final report.

Assessing Specific Areas

Next we will look at each Layer of Security and the types of security questions that should be considered for each area. The provided questions apply principles of Crime Prevention Through Environmental Design (CPTED) and focus on issues pertinent to potential mass casualty incidents.

CPTED is based on the idea that a physical environment can positively influence human behavior through:

- Natural surveillance: Ability to see what is occurring in a particular setting;
- Natural access control: Ability to restrict who enters or exits an environment; and
- Territorial maintenance: Ability to demonstrate ownership of and respect for property.

Checklists for each area assessment are provided at the end of this section.

Assessing Layer 1: Surrounding Neighborhood and Site Location

Your facility exists in relation to the community around it. As you assess this first layer of security, consider:

- Security threats and resources that exist within the neighborhood.
- Marking and security of property lines.

- Traffic patterns.
- Potential hiding places along pedestrian routes. (As an example, in one incident, assailants set off a school fire alarm, then hid in an adjacent wooded area and fired on teachers and students as they evacuated the building.)

Assessing Layer 2: Outdoor Property

As you approach the building, assess outdoor spaces that may affect security. Include:

- Parking and traffic areas.
- Outdoor activity areas such as playgrounds, athletic areas, campus quads, walkways, and other areas where students or members could be at risk.
- Landscaping and lighting.
- Facility surroundings.

Is there anything that would help an assailant with either concealment or building access, or that would put people in greater danger?

Assessing Layer 3a: Building Exterior

Look carefully at the exterior of each building at your facility. Walk around the buildings checking for any means of access, including doors, windows, garage bays, and rooftop access.

- Can the building be accessed from multiple entrances or only one main entrance?
- When are doors kept open, and when are they locked? Are they monitored?
- Are windows accessible from the outside? Can they be used to gain access to the building? Are they protected?
- Is there a roof access?

Assessing Layer 3b: Building Interior

Vulnerability factors vary according to the type of interior space and its typical use. Typical types of areas to assess include:

Entrance Areas:

- Do signs spell out access and check-in requirements?
- Can doors be electronically locked to block an intruder's entry into the building?

- If security screening is used, is there enough space for queuing, equipment, and pulling people aside for more thorough investigation?
- Can internal doors be secured until visitors confer with the receptionist to gain entry?
- Can those in the reception area see the main entry, the drop-off and visitor parking areas, the adjoining halls and stairwells, and, preferably, the closest bathroom entries?
- Does the reception area include protective features and a panic button to call for help?

Open Areas (Auditoriums, Cafeterias, Conference Rooms, Social Areas, Sanctuaries):

- Do open areas have separate, secure, controllable entrances? Can they be locked from either or both sides?
- Are there emergency exits?
- Is there two-way communication between the open area and the main office?
- Do seating and circulation layouts reduce or eliminate traffic flow conflicts?
- Is there a clear view of the entire area from a controlled entry point?
- Are usher/greeters or staff trained in helping people evacuate or seek cover?
- Are there designated helpers for children and those with access and functional needs?

Individual Rooms (Classrooms, Offices, Work Rooms, Childcare Areas):

- Do classroom and office windows provide a view of the site grounds?
- Are there provisions for two-way verbal communication between all classrooms or offices and the administrative or security offices?
- Can each room be quickly locked down from the inside without having to step into the hallway?
- Is there a way (e.g., using master keys or cards) for staff to gain quick entry to any room where individuals have secured themselves?
- Can doors be opened from the inside for emergency exit?
- Are portable classrooms situated for security (e.g., visible from the main building or monitored by closed circuit television cameras, gathered within security fencing, peepholes in doors, included in the public address/intercom system, fitted with doors lockable from inside)?

Passageways:

- Can corridors be monitored by natural or electronic surveillance?
- Is surveillance of stairwells and elevators possible?
- Can interior doors be electronically locked to close off sections of the building?
- Is door hardware on corridor doors resistant to being locked or chained by assailants as a way of significantly slowing down security officers in pursuit?

- Are lockers secured with facility-owned padlocks or electronic pass cards? If locks are used, does the facility retain ownership?

Support Areas:

- Are support areas kept locked when not in use, including, for example:
    - Custodial and equipment rooms and maintenance areas?
    - Kitchens?
    - Staff lounges?
    - Choir rooms?
- Are all rooms containing mechanical, electrical, communications, water, fire, security, and other critical equipment identified by number or simply as "Equipment Room" to provide less information to intruders?
- Are support areas included in surveillance system coverage?

Looking at Operations

The assessment should look beyond the physical attributes of the facility and consider how protective measures are being implemented. For example, it is one thing for doors to be lockable; are they, in fact, kept locked?

Through observation and interviews, assess how access control and visitor management measures are being put into practice.

Operations Questions

- ☐ Is the number of entrance doors that are kept unlocked kept to a minimum?
- ☐ Is it feasible to control and screen people entering the facility? If not, are people assigned to observe who is entering the facility?
- ☐ Are all keys stored securely?
- ☐ Are logs kept for issuing and controlling keys?
- ☐ Do local police and fire departments have access to master keys?
- ☐ Are windows kept locked and secured?
- ☐ Are doors and hallways leading into private areas kept locked, or closed if they must remain unlocked?
- ☐ Is there a formal visitor check-in and identification procedure, and is it clear for first-time visitors, including service personnel and vendors?
- ☐ If there is a visitor check-in procedure, does staff check the identification of any visitor they do not know on sight and issue temporary visitor identifications? Does the identification indicate the destination of each visitor, as well as time and date of visit?
- ☐ Is there an identification system? Are the systems used consistently?

- □ Are designated security personnel (e.g., safety officer, security guard, school resource officer) provided to monitor and attend to issues of security?

Do Not Overlook Special Events

Your vulnerability assessment should extend to special events and activities, both onsite and offsite, and the added challenges they may pose. Examples of special events include the following:

- **Schools:** Sports events, performances, field days, open houses, after-school programs, field trips.
- **Colleges:** Guest speakers, concerts, performances, conferences, sports events, use of campus facilities by outside groups.
- **Houses of worship:** Special ceremonies and services, weddings, funerals, open houses, vacation schools and camps, fundraisers, cook-outs or picnics.

Challenges Sometimes Associated With Special Events

- Focus of the event, and any emotional triggers or controversy associated with it
- Media attention
- Crowd size
- Presence of visitors
- Noise level
- Obstructed views
- Exposure in open spaces
- Transportation and travel-related issues
- Ratio of adults to children
- Overnight arrangements

Security Issues for Special Events

Key issues for special events include:

- Physical security (access control, transportation security)
- Information and communication
    - Alternate methods for external communication (e.g., cell phones, landlines, radios)
    - Alternative methods for internal communication (e.g., PA system, cell phones, handheld radios, bullhorns)
    - Methods for contacting parents
- Emergency procedures (e.g., evacuation, reverse evacuation, lockdown procedures)

Using Assessment Tools

This section has presented an overview of what to look for when assessing each layer. As you get started, you may find that having a comprehensive checklist to guide your assessment would help ensure that all important issues are assessed and that a standard approach is used.

Many different assessment tools are available, covering all aspects of safety, and they can be tailored to your purposes and your setting. The following link provides examples of assessment questions for each layer of security that relate specifically to incidents that could result in mass casualties.

However, it is important to remember that the assessment process is more important than filling out a checklist. Checklists are meant to aid you in being thorough and organized, but they are not the most important part of the process.

Sample Checklists

Layer 1 Security Checklist

	Question	Comments
☐	Do perimeter fences, walls, or "hostile vegetation" provide sufficient access control?	
☐	Are entry points to the site kept to a minimum?	
☐	Are property lines and site entry points clearly marked by fences, landscaping, signs, or other means?	
☐	Can site entry points be seen and monitored in the course of normal activities?	
☐	Can unsupervised site entrances be secured during low-use times for access control purposes?	
☐	Have relationships been established with community watch or other neighborhood-based organizations to foster reporting of suspicious activities?	
☐	Are hiding places minimized or eliminated along pedestrian routes?	

| ☐ | Can traffic patterns be altered to restrict, slow, or monitor cars, buses, and trucks near buildings? | |

Layer 2 Security Checklist

		Question	Comments
Parking and Traffic Areas	☐	Are parking areas within view of the main office, other staffed areas, or surveillance cameras?	
	☐	Is visitor parking located near the main entrance, with clear signs directing visitors to the main office?	
	☐	Is parking for visitors and part-time personnel separated from long-term parking, making it easier to monitor incoming cars?	
	☐	Is there a designated loading/unloading zone for buses and vans that can be seen and monitored?	
	☐	Are parking areas patrolled?	
Outdoor Activity Areas	☐	Can play areas and athletic facilities be observed and monitored from the building?	
	☐	Are play areas protected by clearly defined boundaries, protective barriers, adequate setback from public areas, and emergency escape gates?	
	☐	Are field houses and other outbuildings securable to prevent intruders from gaining entry?	
	☐	Is there an external public address system to notify	

		people in outside areas of an emergency situation?	
Landscaping and Lighting	☐	Consider whether landscaping and exterior lighting contribute to or detract from security. For example:	
	☐	Is the exterior lighting scheme effective for enhancing natural surveillance? (Exterior lighting is best evaluated at night.)	
	☐	Can exterior lighting controls be centrally accessed from the main office?	
	☐	Do the landscaping and lighting allow community members and passing patrol cars to observe and serve as guardians?	
	☐	Do the landscaping and other exterior features prevent climbing onto the roof or through windows?	
	☐	Is the landscaping maintained to minimize hiding places?	
	☐	Is the exterior lighting scheme effective for discouraging trespassing?	
	☐	Are most parking spaces reasonably illuminated at night?	
Facility Surroundings	☐	Are separate wings, separate buildings, and modular classrooms readily identified from a distance by colors, icons, or signage?	
	☐	Are unintended access points (e.g., manholes, utility tunnels, culverts) to the property secured?	

		Question	Comments
	☐	Do bomb threat evacuation sites remain confidential to administrators, staff, and law enforcement?	

Layer 3a: Building Exterior Checklist

		Question	**Comments**
General	☐	Is access into the building(s) 100 percent controllable through designated, supervised, or locked entry points, including windows and service entries?	
	☐	Is entry granted by supervising staff or through the use of proximity cards, keys, coded entries, or other devices?	
	☐	Are there signs, in all relevant languages, directing visitors to designated entrances?	
Exterior Doors and Walls	☐	Are all exterior doors designed to prevent unauthorized access and properly maintained?	
	☐	Are all exit doors and gates equipped with emergency exit hardware and not locked or secured by any other means?	
	☐	Do exterior doors have features that permit seeing who is on the exterior side (e.g., narrow windows, sidelights, fish-eye viewers, or cameras)?	
	☐	Are windows and sidelights sized and located so that if they are broken, intruders cannot reach through and open a door from the inside?	
	☐	Are exterior walls designed to minimize hiding places?	

		Question	Comments
	☐	Do alarms or other systems exist for notifying when doorways are unintentionally left unlocked?	
Windows	☐	Do windows allow observation of courtyards, grounds, and parking lots, especially from administration areas and classrooms?	
	☐	Do all windows lock securely? If used for ventilation, can they be locked half-open?	
	☐	Are windows that serve as a secondary means of escape free of blockage and readily opened from the inside?	
	☐	In high-risk areas, are windows designed and located to resist the effects of explosive blasts, gunfire, and forced entry (e.g., with laminate or security glazing)?	
Roofs	☐	Is the roof accessed only from inside the building?	
	☐	Is access through skylights blocked by security grilles or other devices?	
Court-yards	☐	Are lines of sight across courtyards unobstructed so one person can supervise the entire area?	
	☐	Are entries into courtyards from the exterior of the building controlled and lockable?	

Layer 3b: Building Interior Checklist

		Question	Comments

Entrance Areas	☐	Do signs spell out access and check-in requirements?	
	☐	Can doors be electronically locked to block an intruder's entry into the building?	
	☐	If security screening is used, is there enough space for queuing, equipment, and pulling people aside for more thorough investigation?	
	☐	Can internal doors be secured until visitors confer with the receptionist to gain entry?	
	☐	Can those in the reception area see the main entry, the drop-off and visitor parking areas, the adjoining halls and stairwells, and, preferably, the closest bathroom entries?	
	☐	Does the reception area include protective features and a panic button to call for help?	
Open Areas	☐	Do open areas have separate, secure, controllable entrances? Can they be locked from either or both sides?	
	☐	Are there emergency exits?	
	☐	Is there two-way communication between the open area and the main office?	
	☐	Do seating and circulation layouts reduce or eliminate traffic flow conflicts?	
	☐	Is there a clear view of the entire area from a controlled entry point?	
	☐	Are usher/greeters or staff trained in helping people evacuate or seek cover?	
	☐	Are there designated helpers for children and those with access and functional needs?	

Individual Rooms	☐ Do classroom and office windows provide a view of the site grounds?	
	☐ Are there provisions for two-way verbal communication between all classrooms or offices and the administrative or security offices?	
	☐ Can each room be quickly locked down from the inside without having to step into the hallway?	
	☐ Is there a way (e.g., using master keys or cards) to gain quick entry to any room where individuals have secured themselves?	
	☐ Can doors be opened from the inside for emergency exit?	
	☐ Are portable classrooms situated for security (e.g., visible from the main building or monitored by CCTV cameras, gathered within security fencing, peepholes in doors, included in the PA system, fitted with doors lockable from inside)?	
Passageways	☐ Can corridors be monitored by natural or electronic surveillance?	
	☐ Is surveillance of stairwells and elevators possible?	
	☐ Can interior doors be electronically locked to close off sections of the building?	
	☐ Is door hardware on corridor doors resistant to being locked or chained by assailants as a way of significantly slowing down security officers in pursuit?	
	☐ Are lockers secured with facility-owned padlocks or electronic pass cards? If locks are used, does the facility retain ownership?	
Support Areas	☐ Are support areas kept locked when not in use, including, for example: Custodial and equipment rooms and	

	maintenance areas? Kitchens? Staff lounges? Choir rooms?	
	☐ Are all rooms containing mechanical, electrical, communications, water, fire, security, and other critical equipment identified by number or simply as "Equipment Room" to provide less information to intruders?	
	☐ Are support areas included in surveillance system coverage?	

Fostering a Secure and Safe Environment

Effective security programs foster a broad sense of responsibility and awareness among faculty, staff, and students or members of the congregation.

Security-conscious people regard safety and security as their personal responsibility. They are alert to lapses in security and take steps to correct them. They are observant, make reasonable evaluations of the potential for harm, and when needed, warn others and get help.

It is important for the people who are being protected to understand that security also depends on them and that technological solutions are only effective when people support them.

To be successful, the attitude of shared responsibility needs to extend beyond the walls of your facility and involve the whole community. This includes households, neighbors, social service organizations, local business, responders, community leaders, and others.

Because security begins and ends with the people, effective security programs must build partnerships and promote awareness.

Security Begins and Ends With People

People are your greatest security asset. They are what make your security and safety measures work. For example, an alarm is useless if no one responds to it, or if it is not turned on. A lock is ineffective if a door is propped open.

Effective programs:

- Foster a broad sense of responsibility and security awareness among everyone involved.
- Help participants recognize that they have a personal stake in maintaining a safe environment.
- Empower participants to make a difference through observation, action, and reporting.
- Foster a climate of mutual respect.

Security Tips

- The little things count:
  - A clean environment and simple politeness can enhance safety.
  - Insist that people treat each other the way they want to be treated—with respect, courtesy, and thoughtfulness. Disrespect, when left unchecked, tends to escalate into problems between people.
- Students, employees, members of the congregation, and other stakeholders can provide valuable input in the means used to safeguard them.
  - They can often provide fresh insights into existing problems.
  - They can sometimes spot flawed ideas and avoid wasting precious funds.
  - They can often help build support for measures or programs when we might expect significant resistance.
  - Peer mediation programs, teen courts, and other programs allow individuals to solve problems involving their peers.
- The process of conducting a security assessment can help increase security awareness.

Building on Lessons Learned

Analysis of past incidents has provided insights into ways to make the environment safer and more secure. Lesson 1 discussed a number of lessons from the Safe Schools Initiative—notably that assailants make plans, display observable behaviors prior to the incident, and talk about their plans. Select the information icon below to review the key findings.

Based on these findings, several measures have been proposed to reduce the likelihood of an incident:

- Heighten security awareness.
- Identify warning signs.
- Establish procedures for reporting and investigating threats.
- Identify and assess potential threat indicators.

Safe Schools Initiative Key Findings

The Safe Schools Initiative report included the following key findings:

- Incidents of targeted violence at schools rarely were sudden impulsive acts.
- Most attackers did not threaten their targets directly prior to advancing the attack.
- There was no useful or accurate "profile" of individuals who engaged in targeted violence.
- Most attackers had difficulty coping with significant losses or personal failures. Many had considered or attempted suicide.
- Many attackers felt bullied, persecuted, or injured by others prior to the attack.
- Most attackers had access to and had used weapons prior to the attack.
- Despite prompt law enforcement responses, most shooting incidents were stopped by means other than law enforcement interventions.
- In many cases, others were involved in the incident in some capacity.
- Most attackers engaged in some behavior prior to the incident that caused others concern or indicated a need for help.
- Prior to the incidents, other people knew about the attacker's idea and/or plan to attack.

Heightening Security Awareness

A heightened security awareness depends on making people aware of, and partners in, your security policies and procedures. For example, is everyone at your site prepared to:

- Help control access to the building (keeping doors locked, not blocking them open, not holding doors open for unauthorized persons)?
- Help enforce visitor management by identifying possible trespassers? (A simple "May I help you find your way?" can be used to steer individuals to the check-in site.)
- Notice and report lapses in the physical environment that could affect safety?
- Help reduce behaviors such as bullying or intimidation that detract from a climate of respect?

Willingness to engage people as security partners in these ways relies on having established a climate of trust.

Tip: Getting Input

Surveys are a useful tool for gaining input from those in your organization. The team should survey the community (students, staff, parents/guardians, volunteers, members of the congregation) to find out what concerns they may have and how aware they are of programs and systems that are in place. Remember that perceptions are potent and may influence people as much as reality.

Examples of Programs That Work

Teen Community Emergency Response Team (CERT), a CitizenCorps program, was created to address preparedness and response capabilities from within high schools. Teen CERT aims to train students in emergency preparedness and basic response to ensure that they have the skills needed to protect themselves, and assist others, in the event of an emergency.

In addition to providing assistance as needed during actual emergencies, trained students may support other activities within the school. They may point out unsafe conditions, help in evacuations like fire drills, identify students who have become disenfranchised, or serve as role models who take on new leadership responsibilities within the school.

Students Against Violence Everywhere (SAVE) is a student-initiated program to promote nonviolence. SAVE recognizes that young people can take part in making schools and communities safer by focusing on crime prevention, conflict management, and service projects. SAVE students provide positive peer influences to prevent violence.

SAVE encourages and empowers students by giving them a voice in violence prevention, providing them with knowledge and skills to provide service, and educating them about the consequences of violence and the impact of safe activities.

Warning Signs

The Secret Service found that people who need help often do not keep it a secret. They may exhibit obvious warning signs either through behavior or remarks, such as voicing problems or grievances, showing signs of depression or desperation, or planning out their attacks.

Participants in a security culture should be alert to such signs and recognize their potential significance.

In 2007, several months prior to killing five people at two locations (a church and youth program) in Colorado Springs, Colorado, a former member of the youth program began posting disturbing messages to a Web site including a poem that spurred a psychologist to offer help. And just a few weeks prior to his killing spree, the gunman sent hate mail to the youth program.

Examples of Potential Warning Behaviors

- **Research, planning, and preparation for an attack,** such as researching how to build a bomb, sketching maps and diagrams, or making lists of targets.
- **Attempts to obtain a weapon.**
- **Suicidal threats and attempts.** In one case, a student wrote several poems for English class that involved themes of homicide and suicide as possible solutions to feelings of hopelessness.
- **Difficulty coping with significant losses or personal failures.** Depression or desperation over romantic breakups, death of a loved one, loss of status, job loss, divorce, or academic failure all have been linked to violent episodes.
- **History of being bullied, threatened, harassed, or attacked.**
- **Inappropriate interest in accounts or themes of mass violence.** Some attackers expressed great admiration for prior mass killings in the news, or glorified violence their own writings.

Reporting Procedures

In a study by the Secret Service and Department of Education, bystanders (people who had knowledge of mass casualty incidents before they occurred) were interviewed. The study concluded that **information learned may prevent a targeted attack.** The study highlighted the importance of:

- Establishing a climate where individuals are encouraged to come forward with information about threats and other concerning behavior, without fearing punishment, ridicule, or not being taken seriously.
- Developing policies on threat reporting and training for adults in how to properly respond to such information.

Policy Recommendations

The bystander study recommended that school policies should:

- Encourage students, staff, faculty, parents, and others to report all apparent threats or threatening or disturbing behaviors. They must be motivated to report threats, know what to report, and how to do it. Posters, signs, videos, assemblies, and workshops can be used to let people know how much their safety depends on their willingness to get involved.
- Provide several options for the reporting of threats, including reporting anonymously if necessary.
- Ensure that all those who report a threat or threatening situation will be treated with respect and that the information they provide will be closely guarded.

- Emphasize that the school will take appropriate action on all reports and will, within the confines of privacy laws, provide feedback to the reporting student that the information was received, and that appropriate action was taken.
- Articulate what types of student information and knowledge can be shared, with whom it can be shared, and under what conditions it can be shared.
- Be clear as to who is responsible for acting on information received regarding threats.
- Where the law permits, include law enforcement and mental health officials in the review process.
- Track threats over time so that the information collected regarding threats can be used in the decisionmaking process.

Potential Threat Indicators

There is no profile or set of risk factors with which to reliably identify the next offender. A number of factors in a person's life may influence the propensity for violence, but oversimplification is likely to misidentify threats.

The Secret Service, FBI, and other organizations recommend, instead, an organized **threat assessment process** conducted by trained professionals. Threat assessment uses a set of strategies to determine the credibility and seriousness of a threat and the likelihood that it will be carried out.

The Threat Assessment Process

The threat assessment process recommended by the Secret Service, FBI, and others:

- Should be done by an interdisciplinary team of trained professionals that includes law enforcement, social services and mental health providers, and others in the community that can contribute to the threat assessment.
- Should be supported by clear policy and protocols for exploring allegations of actual or potential violence.
- Depends on a climate of trust between youth and adults.
- Consists of evaluating a threat, reaching a conclusion regarding threat level, and determining an effective response.
- Involves:
    - Assessing the threat's type and level of risk.
    - Considering all factors shaping the individual's decisionmaking and actions, including personality and behavior, school dynamics, social dynamics, and home dynamics.
    - Determining and implementing interventions in a timely manner.

    o   Providing supportive interventions to potential offenders.

Programs That Work

In partnership with mental health, law enforcement, and juvenile justice agencies, the **Clark County Schools (NV) Student Threat Assessment Program** provides Student Threat Assessment services to school districts in Clark County. Services include:

- Training of key staff in schools regarding the Level I in-building threat screening process of students or situations of concern.
- Coordination of Level II threat assessments in which a trained multidisciplinary team comes to a school site, assesses risk, and assists in management and intervention planning.
- Preparation of timely written threat assessment summaries following the Level II assessment process.

Clark County Student Threat Assessment

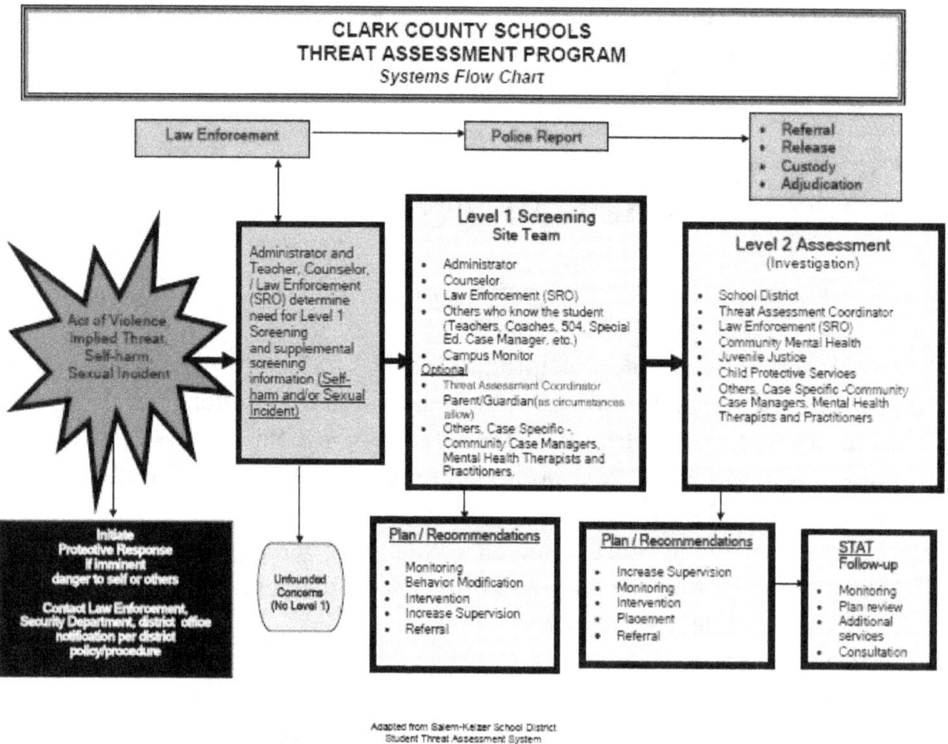

More information is available from:
http://web3.esd112.org/teaching-and-learning/prevention/threatassessment

Engaging the Whole Community

The public has long served as the "eyes and ears" of their communities. Community members:

- Act as force multipliers.
- Are a critical resource in maintaining a safe environment for education and worship.
- Contribute to security by being alert and reporting situations that could impact safety in schools, places of worship, and other institutions in the community.

By building on the community partnerships begun during the planning process, you can engage the whole community in improving your organization's security.

Tips for Engaging the Community

There are many ways to engage the community in the process of safety planning. There are also many ways to engage the community on an ongoing basis in programs and strategies that will help make your organization safer.

- Involve community members on the planning team.
- Gather their feedback through surveys.
- Involve them through a forum.
- Consult them as needed for expertise.
- Ask for their support of measures.
- Broaden your outreach by making use of Web sites and television and radio channels operated by school districts, universities, and faith-based organizations

Parent and Caregiver Contributions:

- Program development and implementation
- Cultural/diversity programming
- Mentoring and volunteering (can serve as hallway, playground, and lunchroom monitors)
- Visitor check-in table
- Safety patrols to and from school
- Advocacy to elected officials and school board

Community Service Provider Contributions:

- Identifying learning and behavioral problems
- Counseling
- Resolving conflicts and providing alternatives to violence
- Conducting parent education programs

- Teaching social skills
- Providing afterschool and in-school programming
- Providing safe havens for kids

Community Campaigns That Work

"If You See Something, Say Something™" Campaign – The "If You See Something, Say Something™" campaign encourages citizens to be more aware of their surroundings and to report suspicious activity, behavior, or packages to law enforcement. Posters, videos, and audio clips are available to local organizations to aid their efforts to promote suspicious activity awareness and reporting. The "If You See Something, Say Something™" video available on the DHS Web site is a valuable educational tool to teach community members about types of suspicious activities and explains the process by which reports are processed. (http://www.dhs.gov/if-you-see-something-say-something)

Ready Campaign – The Ready Campaign is a national public service advertising campaign designed to educate and empower Americans to prepare for emergencies. The goal is to get the public involved and ultimately to increase the level of preparedness across the Nation. The campaign encourages the public to get an emergency kit, make an emergency plan, and be informed about what protective measures to take before, during, and after any type of disaster. (http://www.ready.gov/)

Addressing Safety and Security Vulnerabilities

After identifying potential vulnerabilities, it is important to develop practical strategies for enhancing protective measures.

The team works together by asking:

- What can we do to avert dangerous situations?
- How can we protect our people and lessen the negative consequences if an incident occurs?
- What is appropriate for **our** organization?

Answers to these questions help teams to consider and select the strategies for reducing vulnerabilities.

These strategies may include simple changes such as modifying landscaping, improving lighting, or adding signs.

Other improvements may involve enhancing locks, window protection, or communications systems. And, in some cases, adding surveillance technology may be warranted.

In addition to physical changes, updated policies and procedures may be needed and incorporated into the all-hazards emergency operations plan or other documents.

Remember, there are numerous resources and experts within the community who are willing and available to help.

Security Measures

Below are potential types of security measures:

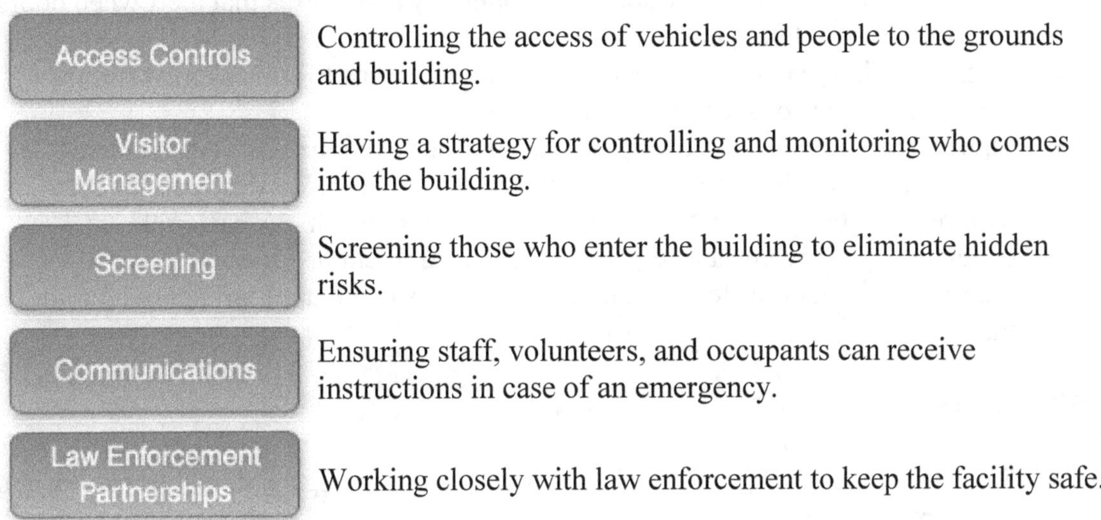

Controlling the access of vehicles and people to the grounds and building.

Having a strategy for controlling and monitoring who comes into the building.

Screening those who enter the building to eliminate hidden risks.

Ensuring staff, volunteers, and occupants can receive instructions in case of an emergency.

Working closely with law enforcement to keep the facility safe.

Addressing Vulnerabilities

After identifying potential vulnerabilities, it is important to develop practical strategies for enhancing protective measures. If your situation is like most, the existing building structure and budgetary restrictions may limit how elaborate your solutions can be. However, thinking creatively may reveal a wide array of security alternatives that are very cost effective. Examples include:

- Using environmental solutions to improve access control.
- Developing procedures to improve security, and consistently enforcing existing protocols.
- Taking advantage of in-house capabilities to correct physical vulnerabilities.

- Combining technology solutions with simple, low-tech alternatives.
- Partnering with the community to develop shared strategies.

Examples of Protective Measures

Access control:

- Do not forget the need to educate students, staff, parents/guardians, and congregants about access control procedures.
- Use environmental control measures, such as landscaping, signs, posters, and diagrams, to channel people into the check-in area.
- Make it difficult to park an unauthorized vehicle close to a building.
- Minimize the number of open entrances to the building (lock doors when they do not need to be open).
- Make improvements in landscaping, such as removing objects that might restrict visibility through windows to the outside.
- Install mechanisms that lock doors automatically and alarms that alert when doors are inadvertently left open.
- Consider using features such as buzzers and intercoms to control entry through the main entrance or secondary inner doors.
- Many organizations look toward the use of security equipment (e.g., cameras, metal detectors) to ensure safety. However, even excellent safety equipment requires with the "human touch" to deliver optimal results. A basic rule is to understand your needs before you purchase equipment or services. Assess security equipment for features, effectiveness, cost, and appropriateness for your facility.

Visitor management:

- Set up visitor screening protocols that include sign-in, sign-out, visitor passes, and escort procedures.
- Require service people, suppliers, and vendors to abide by the screening protocols.
- Use identification methods such as photo identification for staff and, if appropriate, learners or members. Some places of worship have name badges for those who attend regularly, to help greeters and others identify (and welcome) new faces. These badges also have value for security purposes.
- Provide training in how to engage unrecognized individuals and guide them toward visitor check-in.
- Consider electronic systems such as badge entry systems and proximity badges for staff.

Screening:

- Train staff, greeters and ushers, and other volunteers in visual weapons screening techniques to spot suspicious activity and persons carrying a weapon. Violators will often give observable cues because of the discomfort caused by carrying the weapon, fear of being caught, or the weight, size, or shape of the weapon. This approach has been used to successfully avert a number of planned attacks.

- Screen all persons who enter the facility after hours.
- If warranted, consider a random weapons screening program, selecting classrooms or school bus numbers randomly for screening.
- Screen all new staff hires. Careful examination of work history and criminal records can help reduce risk. Require multiple work references, interview each one, and consider pre-employment drug screening. Do not forget contract employees, substitutes, temporary workers, and even volunteers in the screening process.
- Consider barring certain individuals from the premises, such as suspended and expelled students or persons with a past record of violent behavior.

Communications:

- Enable the main office to notify all areas of the facility in the event of an emergency.
- The use of codes for initiating response actions is discouraged because of the confusion they can create. If code words or phrases are used, make them simple, clear, and easily remembered, and familiarize all staff members (including temporary staff and volunteers) with them.
- Be sure outdoor areas such as playgrounds can receive notifications.
- Provide redundant means of requesting emergency assistance.
- Provide for two-way communications between the main office and other areas.
- Enhance radio systems to ensure interoperability with local law enforcement.

A law enforcement partnership:

- Cultivate partnerships with law enforcement for joint analysis, planning, and cooperation to identify security strategies, such as:
  - Joint monitoring of activities.
  - Surveillance patrols.
  - School resource officer (SRO) programs. SROs bring a heightened awareness of warning signs and cues relevant in threat assessment. They can provide instruction about the consequences of their behavior and identify peer conflicts. In times of crisis, having an SRO based in the school decreases response time and increases student and staff perceptions of safety.

Programs That Work

The **Bibb County Public School System** in Georgia developed a program to train selected custodians to serve in a special safety role, as additional eyes and ears for school administrators and campus police. As safety specialists, they were responsible for reporting and coordinating rather than confronting potentially dangerous situations directly. Training prepared them to:

- Function as relief crossing guards.
- Use visual screening techniques to spot persons who are carrying a gun on or near campus.
- Conduct a sweep of the building for suspicious packages that could contain an explosive device or a delivery system for a chemical/biological weapon.
- Help to evacuate the building during a crisis.
- Help to manage parking at the reunification center during a crisis at another school in the district.
- Constantly monitor the school for any type of safety hazard.
- Serve on the school safety committee.
- Make suggestions to improve the level of safety at the school.

Southern Arkansas University implemented the Adopt-a-Cop program to reduce crime in campus residence halls. The program assigns a specific police officer to each residence hall and apartment complex. In addition to patrolling an assigned area, the assigned officer communicates with the director of the residence hall, is available to speak with residents on safety concerns, and conducts safety programs for students.

Harts Bluff Independent School District implemented the Watch D.O.G.S. (Dads of Great Students) program that invites fathers, grandfathers, uncles, or other father figures to volunteer one day each school year to monitor entrances and perimeters, load or unload buses, work with coaches, or help in the cafeteria or a classroom. Each volunteer is screened with a criminal background check and then provided with an overview of the campus, rules to follow, a schedule, and a hand-held radio.

Updating Policies, Procedures, and Plans

In addition to physical changes, updated policies and procedures may be needed. The next lesson provides detailed information on the most common procedures related to responding to and recovering from mass casualty incidents.

Remember, it is important to make sure that all new or revised procedures are incorporated into the all-hazards emergency operations plan or other documents and that personnel must be trained on the new and revised procedures.

Resources

You can use the following resources to learn more about assessing vulnerabilities, fostering a secure and safe environment, and addressing security vulnerabilities.

Assessing Vulnerabilities

- Federal Emergency Management Agency (FEMA) Risk Management Series.
- Department of Homeland Security (DHS) Building and Infrastructure Protection Series Tools.
- National Clearinghouse for Educational Facilities.
- American Clearinghouse on Educational Facilities.
- Readiness and Emergency Management for School, Technical Assistance Center.
- Anti-Defamation League Security.
- National Association of School Psychologists (NASP) Resources.

Fostering a Secure and Safe Environment

- United States Secret Service National Threat Assessment Center.
- Community Emergency Response Teams (CERT).
- Students Against Violence Everywhere (SAVE).
- Federal Bureau of Investigation (FBI) Reports and Publications.
- U.S. Department of Education, Emergency Planning, Office of Safe and Healthy Students.
- Department of Justice, Office of Juvenile Justice and Delinquency Prevention Publications.
- National Crime Prevention Council.
- Department of Homeland Security, If You See Something, Say Something™.
- Ready Campaign (FEMA).

Addressing Security Vulnerabilities

- Anti-Defamation League Security.
- National Criminal Justice Reference Service.
- Readiness and Emergency Management for School, Technical Assistance Center.
- CPTED 101. Crime Prevention through Environmental Design—The Fundamentals for Schools.

Lesson Summary

You should now understand the importance of making your environment more secure by identifying your site's vulnerabilities, fostering a secure and safe environment, and initiating measures that address security vulnerabilities.

The next lesson addresses how to respond in the event of an emergency.

Lesson 4: During an Incident

During an Incident: Implementing Established Response Procedures

This lesson will describe the types of response procedures to establish for a mass casualty incident.

At the completion of this lesson, you should be able to identify:

- Immediate response actions to take in a potential mass casualty incident.
- Types and uses of response procedures for responding to a potential mass casualty incident.
- Lessons learned from responses to past incidents.

During an Incident

It's looking like a typical day. First the rush of people arriving, then a few stragglers, and now the normal hum of a regular schedule underway. And then the intercom sounds. A staff member has encountered a suspicious situation, a lockdown is called, and you can hear shouting. Would you be ready?

The goal of preparedness is to avert situations that could cause harm and to be ready to respond if an incident does occur. Past mass casualty incidents have shown that it is the people onsite who will be the first responders.

The first critical seconds of an incident provide the best opportunity to reduce the loss of human life once an incident occurs. Being ready to act requires having made safety-related decisions in advance, having procedures in place to respond quickly and minimize harm, and having properly trained personnel who are empowered to act quickly in an emergency.

In this lesson you will learn about actions that can be used to enhance safety and factors to consider when planning for response.

Planning for Response

Analysis of mass casualty incidents that have occurred in schools and places of worship has shown that such crises are over quickly—sometimes in a matter of minutes or less. A crisis is not the time to make a plan; it is a time to follow a plan. Quick action can save lives.

During an incident, people need to know how to reduce their risk and protect themselves until help arrives. They need to know:

- **What** to do.
- **When** and **where** to do it.
- **Who** is responsible for what, and what their individual roles are.
- **How** to communicate with others.

Developing a Plan That Is Right for You

No two settings are alike. Differences in the physical site and the population served will influence what kind of response plan is right for your organization.

Many experienced practitioners have contributed ideas about how to respond in a crisis. This lesson will summarize key findings and recommendations from a variety of sources. Select the link below to view key research sources.

Understanding the range of action options and the variables that will affect their effectiveness can help you tailor a response plan to your organization's needs.

Initial Response Action Steps

As soon as a dangerous situation becomes evident, several things need to happen:

- Assess the situation, choose the appropriate response, and take immediate action.
- Take action to protect yourself first so you can in turn protect others.
- Take action to protect those in your immediate area.
- Communicate the need for others to take immediate protective actions.
- Notify emergency responders.
- Initiate the chosen response action and related emergency protocols found in your plan.
- Triage injuries and apply emergency first aid as needed.

Assessing the Situation

A crisis plan provides the framework and overall procedures for responding to a crisis, but it cannot provide a roadmap sufficient to cover the details of every incident that might occur.

Individual judgment will be needed about what you can and should do first, keeping in mind that the primary goal is taking care of people at risk and minimizing harm. Taking action to protect yourself may make it possible to in turn protect others. The choice of appropriate response actions will depend on the situation and your local conditions. Key factors include:

Type of Event

The type of event is one factor that will drive the appropriate response. Actions that could save lives in one situation could cause death if applied in a different situation. For example:

- Weapon reported—Some of the most common weapons situations are those where a weapon has been reported or detected. If people misread this situation and react with an approach that might be appropriate when confronted by an armed aggressor, an avoidable weapons assault may be created.
- Threats or brandishing a weapon—If a weapon has not yet been used, proper handling could keep the situation from turning deadly. Aggressive reactions could easily result in a weapon being used.
- Suicide threat with a weapon—The person could decide to open fire on others. At the same time, care must be taken not to take actions that could make the situation worse, such as trying to disarm a person pointing a gun.
- Active shooter—Although such incidents can involve mass casualties, they are also rare and should not be the only focus of prevention and preparedness.
- Hostage situation—Avoiding harm to the hostages is a key factor.

Weapons Used

Be careful to not limit your thinking to incidents involving firearms. Attacks using edged weapons (knives, box cutters, etc.), blunt instruments (baseball bats, hammers), explosive devices, or other types of weapons need to be considered and factored into the response.

Characteristics of the Population

The unique needs of those at your site must be considered. All response actions must take into account mental, physical, motor, developmental, and sensory factors. For instance:

- Young children or infants are easily upset and may be difficult to keep quiet.
- Young children also often "freeze" when they are frightened.

- Individuals with limited mobility such as those in wheelchairs or with other auxiliary aids may have difficulty getting to safe locations (e.g., using an evacuation route over a gravel surface) or assuming protective positions. Identify alternative routes or locations for those who may need them and be sure to share with the first responders.
- Individuals with hearing, visual, or cognitive impairments may require alternative methods of emergency notification or assistance in carrying out security measures.
- Some individuals with disabilities react very strongly to loud noises such as a fire alarm.
- Language barriers for non-native English speakers can create challenges.

Characteristics of the Site

Each site will have different characteristics that can impact the response, including how quickly responders get there and who responds. For example:

- It may take longer for first responders to arrive in rural locations.
- Small facilities are more easily and quickly explored by an intruder.
- If flight becomes a viable option, hazards in the surrounding area need to be considered, such as urban traffic, treacherous terrain, or water hazards.
- Internal aspects of the site also become a factor in relation to where within the facility the event is unfolding. For example, if there are multiple buildings, options for protecting people may vary depending on their proximity to the danger. The options in a building with multiple wings will be different from those in a compact building with one main corridor, or with a centralized open space such as in a place of worship.

Choosing Response Actions

Depending on the situation, getting people to safety may be accomplished in different ways. Response actions commonly suggested by the emergency management community include:

Evacuation	Leaving the building if doing so would be safer than remaining inside. Evacuations may be full or partial (e.g., a part of the building away from the action).
Reverse evacuation	Moving people into the facility from an unprotected outside location.
Preventive lockdown	A limited lockdown for use where there is no indication of imminent danger but a heightened level of security may prevent a situation from escalating.
Emergency lockdown	Moving to portions of the building that can be secured, locking doors, and remaining out of sight. Various degrees of lockdown are possible.

| **Seeking shelter** | Hiding behind protective barriers, especially when caught in open spaces where evacuation and lockdown are not possible. |
| **Room clear** | Moving people to a safer location within the facility in a prompt and organized manner. |

Evacuation

Based on the situation, it may be determined that the best way to keep people safe is to evacuate them from the building. Evacuation may be appropriate:

- When occupants are able to determine where aggressor(s) are located.
- When it is unsafe to stay in the building because of an imminent danger, fire, or structural damage.
- When the physical space does not allow for a reasonably effective lockdown.
- When locations outside are safer than inside.
- When the evacuation route does not expose the evacuees to danger.
- In situations where it is safe to evacuate from unaffected parts of the building or campus.

Plans should clearly identify routes, locations, and procedures and include provisions for those with access and functional needs. Drills that provide practice opportunities are important.

Evacuation Planning Considerations

Description: When conditions inside make it unsafe to remain in a building, the safest course of action may be to move people to a safe location outside the building. In certain situations, partial evacuation may be possible, such as when the location of an aggressor is known and portions of the building or campus have a safe route out that does not expose evacuees to danger. In some cases, a law enforcement-led evacuation will be carried out while an incident is still in progress.

When used: Evacuation may be appropriate:

- When occupants are able, to a reasonable extent, to determine where aggressor(s) are located. There have been past incidents where evacuees have run into attackers while trying to evacuate.
- When it is unsafe to stay in the building.
- When the physical space does not allow for a reasonably effective lockdown (e.g., in an area with cubicles with no doors or a classroom pod with no lockable space).
- When locations outside are safer than inside.

- When the evacuation route does not expose the evacuees to danger (e.g., from sniper fire).
- In situations where it is safe to evacuate from unaffected parts of the building or campus.

Considerations for planning:

- Locations and routes:
  - Pre-designate evacuation site locations: safe locations a good distance from the facility. Work with law enforcement to determine evacuation areas.
  - Identify multiple evacuation routes.
  - Prepare site maps with evacuation routes indicated.
  - Maintain evacuation routes in clear condition.
  - Consider evacuation routes for those with access and functional needs (e.g., selecting routes that are navigable by individuals in wheelchairs).
- Procedures should indicate:
  - Decision factors for initiating full or partial evacuation.
  - Conditions under which partial evacuations may be initiated by staff or trained volunteers.
  - Who has responsibility for taking the emergency kits.
  - Procedures for:
    - Initiating an evacuation (e.g., announcements).
    - Conducting an evacuation before law enforcement arrives.
    - Conducting a law enforcement-led evacuation.
    - Accounting for people after the evacuation.
    - Evacuating individuals requiring assistance (e.g., assigned responsibilities, buddy system). Ensure you know who is onsite that would need assistance.

Reverse Evacuation

Reverse evacuation is used to rapidly and safely move people inside a facility when it would be dangerous to remain outside. Reverse evacuation may be appropriate when:

- People are located outside, such as on playgrounds, on sports fields, or at an outdoor event.
- The danger, such as an armed aggressor, is outside.

Unless you have procedures in place for reverse evacuation, you may not be able to execute a lockdown when people remain outside.

Reverse Evacuation Planning Considerations

Description: When the source of danger is outside, and there are people in outdoor areas, reverse evacuation is used to bring them into the safer environment of the building.

When used: Reverse evacuation may be appropriate when:

- It is safer to be inside the building than outside.
- Danger, such as an armed aggressor or other potentially dangerous situation, is located outside the building.
- Groups of people from the facility are located outside and a lockdown is being implemented.

Considerations for planning:

- Procedures should indicate:
    - Decision factors for initiating a reverse evacuation.
    - Conditions under which reverse evacuations may be initiated by those supervising outdoor groups.
    - How people can be informed of the need to conduct a reverse evacuation (for example, by an external public address system).
    - Indoor destinations and routes inside for specific outdoor areas.
    - Procedures for:
        - Initiating a reverse evacuation (e.g., announcements).
        - Ensuring that everyone is inside and accounted for.
        - Helping individuals who require assistance (e.g., assigned responsibilities, buddy system). Ensure you know who is onsite that would need assistance.

Preventive Lockdown

There are times when remaining inside the building is the safest alternative. In a preventive lockdown, perimeter doors are locked to keep a situation from escalating. Preventive lockdown is a realistic option for the numerous situations that can quickly escalate into an emergency unless security is immediately increased.

A preventive lockdown allows for limited normal activities to take place, such as continued teaching within locked rooms. Movement in hallways and other areas is stopped while the situation is investigated and addressed.

Preventive Lockdown Planning Considerations

Description: For K-12 schools, the majority of situations that require a lockdown do not involve a person brandishing or using a weapon. A preventive lockdown involves locking perimeter doors and internal doors to keep a situation from escalating. Limited normal activities such as teaching may continue, but hallway activity ceases. For example, teachers can continue to teach with their rooms locked. Movement in hallways and other areas is stopped while the situation is investigated and addressed.

(Note: Preventive lockdown should not be confused with shelter-in-place, which is used when there is a hazardous condition outside (e.g., a chemical, radiological, or biological hazard) that requires occupants to remain in designated indoor shelter areas, perhaps for an extended period of time, and may involve sealing the room.)

When used:

- When imminent danger is not indicated but there is a need for increased security (for example, if a belligerent person is causing a disturbance in the main office).

Considerations for planning:

- Seek input from emergency responders on your procedures and locations.
- Identify:
  - Locations within the facility that can be secured.
  - For unsecurable locations in the facility, nearby safe havens.
- Procedures should indicate:
  - Decision factors in selecting preventive lockdown as an appropriate response action.
  - Who has responsibility for initiating a preventive lockdown.
  - Training and empowering staff to initiate a lockdown independently, followed by communication to prompt a lockdown for the rest of the building and notification of law enforcement.
  - Procedures for:
    - Initiating a preventive lockdown.
    - Notifying personnel in the facility.
    - Immediate notification of 911 and on-site security and/or law enforcement officers when a lockdown is implemented.
    - Implementing lockdown of individual rooms.
    - Communications between individual rooms and main office.
    - Indicating lockdown status of individual rooms.
    - Accounting for people during the lockdown.
    - Issuing keys to those who will need them.
    - Handling a fire alarm during a lockdown. (Fire alarms should NOT be activated as a response action for an intruder situation.)
    - Notifying occupants' households of the lockdown status.
  - Other considerations:
    - Planning for individuals requiring assistance (e.g., assigned responsibilities, buddy system, posting daily schedules). Ensure you know who is on site that would need assistance and where they will be.

- Precautionary steps such as having internal doors locked as the default.

Emergency Lockdown

During an emergency lockdown, people move quickly to (or remain in) predetermined locations that are relatively secure, and lock the doors. Normal activities cease, and all reasonable means of staying quiet and out of sight are used, according to established procedures. People stay in hiding until help arrives.

Emergency lockdown may be appropriate:

- When evacuation is not a safe alternative.
- When a potentially dangerous person is inside the building, or the situation is unclear.

Emergency Lockdown Planning Considerations

Description: Emergency lockdown is a protective action that involves locking and hiding. When an emergency lockdown is initiated, people move quickly to (or stay within) locations that are relatively secure, and lock the doors. All reasonable means of staying out of sight are used, according to established procedures, which may include turning off lights, getting out of view of windows, turning off cell phones, and remaining quiet. There have been past incidents in which lockdown procedures saved lives, as assailants looking for potential victims simply walked by locked-down rooms.

When used:

- When sounds similar to gunshots are heard inside or near the facility.
- When there is any indication that a person is brandishing or using a weapon inside or in close proximity outside the facility.
- When a report is received that some type of weapons assault is about to occur.
- When evacuation does not appear to be a safe alternative based on the information at hand.

Considerations for planning:

- Seek input from emergency responders on your procedures and locations.
- Identify:
    - Locations within the facility that can be secured.
    - For unsecurable locations in the facility, nearby safe havens.
    - "Safe rooms" for key areas of the facility. For example, if staff in the main office have a rapidly lockable area in the office with a telephone and a connection to the public address system, they can quickly secure

themselves in the room, protect themselves from danger, and make the necessary notifications.
- Procedures should indicate:
  - Decision factors in selecting emergency lockdown as an appropriate response action.
  - Who has responsibility for initiating an emergency lockdown.
  - Training and empowering staff to initiate a lockdown independently, followed by communication to prompt a lockdown for the rest of the building and notification of law enforcement.
  - A method for rapidly moving to evacuation if required (e.g., in case of fire).
  - Procedures for:
    - Initiating a lockdown.
    - Notifying personnel in the facility.
    - Notifying 911 and on-site security and/or law enforcement officers when a lockdown is implemented.
    - Implementing lockdown of individual rooms.
    - Communications between individual rooms and main office.
    - Indicating lockdown status of individual rooms.
    - Accounting for people during the lockdown.
    - Issuing keys to those who will need them.
    - Handling a fire alarm during a lockdown. (Fire alarms should NOT be activated as a response action for an intruder situation.)
    - Notifying occupants' households of the lockdown status.
  - Guidelines for specific situations, such as:
    - Someone seeking refuge after a room has been locked down.
    - Use of cell phones during lockdown.
    - Locations with infants and very young children.
  - Other considerations:
    - Planning for individuals requiring assistance (e.g., assigned responsibilities, buddy system, posting daily schedules). Ensure you know who is on site that would need assistance and where they will be.
    - Preparing and placing supplies for extended lockdowns.
    - Precautionary steps such as having internal doors locked as the default.

Room Clear

The room clear protocol is a standardized procedure that allows personnel to instruct occupants to quickly leave the area and seek shelter in a secure area. This option allows a staff member or trained volunteer to clear people from an area without creating a general evacuation. Each room or area of the building should have a designated shelter room or buddy room so people know where to go if a room clear is issued.

Room clear may be appropriate when:

- Danger is present within the facility and a room or area cannot be secured.
- There is imminent danger to those in the area.
- An aggressive or disruptive person may endanger others in the area.
- A medical emergency has occurred.
- A general evacuation may increase danger but it is not safe for people to remain in a specific area.

Room Clear Planning Considerations

Description: Room clear procedures allow for staff or trained volunteers to carry out an orderly process of emptying a room or area and directing them to an alternate, safer location within the building.

When used: Room clear may be appropriate when:

- Danger is present within the facility and a room or area cannot be secured.
- It is less safe to order a general evacuation of the facility.
- There is imminent danger to those in the area.
- An aggressive or disruptive person may endanger others in the area.
- A medical emergency has occurred and bystanders need to be cleared from the area.

Considerations for planning:

- Develop procedures that address:
  - Decision factors in initiating room clear.
  - Who has responsibility for initiating a room clear.
  - Steps to be followed and instructions to be used when clearing a room.
  - Informing the main office that a room has been cleared.
  - Using standardized language so the need to implement a room clear can be rapidly communicated.
- Other considerations:
  - Planning for individuals requiring assistance (e.g., assigned responsibilities, buddy system). Ensure you know who is onsite that would need assistance.
  - Preparing and placing supplies for extended sheltering.

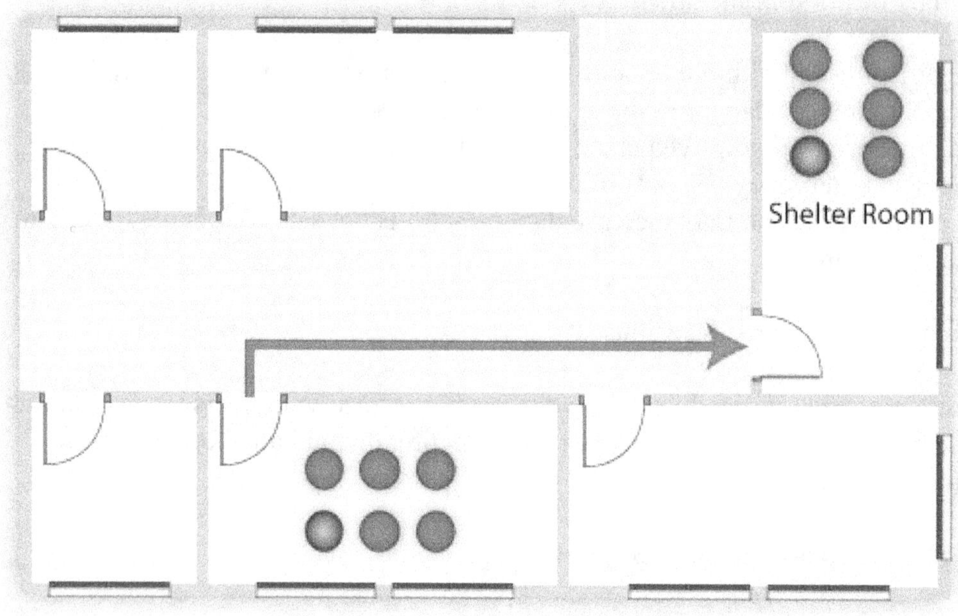

Addressing Nonstandard Situations

When developing response procedures, be sure to consider how nonstandard situations will be handled, such as:

- **Vulnerable times:** What if an incident erupts when people are moving between classes, or leaving the main worship area, or gathered outside?
- **Vulnerable areas:** Are there areas of the facility that require special attention because they afford little or no protective coverage? For example, in a lockdown, what should people in the cafeteria or assembly hall do? Building occupants should be taught to take protective actions such as **seeking shelter** behind protective barriers and staying out of sight if they cannot safely reach a secured area.
- **Autonomous decisions:** There have been times when the first indication of a crisis was a gunshot or screaming rather than an official notification. Under what circumstances are personnel expected to make autonomous decisions about response actions to protect people in their care? Those present at the scene may need to make rapid decisions with little information, and there may not be time to consult a supervisor.

Notification and Communication

When an incident occurs, notification and communication are critical and often need to occur within seconds:

- **Inform the staff or volunteers what response actions are to be taken.** Prompt communication ensures the appropriate safety measures can be taken to protect all the people on site.
- **Notify law enforcement as soon as possible.** It is better to have emergency responders on the scene, even if the incident has been resolved, rather than risk injury.

Notification and Communication Tips

- Take action to protect yourself and other building occupants before you call 911. Calling 911 first can result in protective actions being implemented too late to do any good if one person has to call 911 and communicate the need for protective actions.
- Call 911 as soon as possible. Clearly state the following:
  - Name and address of the incident location.
  - Location of the intruder.
  - Number of intruders, if more than one.
  - Physical description of intruder(s).
  - Number and type of weapon(s).
  - Number of potential victims.
- If communicating with the assailant:
  - Use nonthreatening language and demeanor.
  - Avoid anything that could escalate the situation.
  - Be clear and specific.
- When developing communication procedures:
  - Indicate how staff or trained volunteers will be notified. Use procedures that will not escalate the situation.
  - Use simple, clear language. Plain language is preferred over codes. The use of codes often causes incorrect responses under stress.
  - Indicate who has responsibility for notification, and what to do if that person is not available.
  - Be sure there is a way to notify all areas of your facility, including outside areas.
  - Include provisions for two-way communication between main office and individual rooms.
  - Address how a return to normal operations will be announced.

Triage and Emergency First Aid

If a crisis happens, those onsite may need to give emergency first aid to injured people.

To make this possible, people at your site should be trained in emergency first aid, including stopping bleeding, administering CPR, and use of automated external defibrillators (AEDs). Emergency first aid supplies need to be on hand. Consider:

- Coordinating with local emergency responders on first aid training and emergency supply kit contents.
- Designating a first aid team using trained staff members or volunteers.
- Providing first aid training to groups of students or members of your congregation. First aid training may be available through the American Red Cross, some local fire departments, and as part of Community Emergency Response Team (CERT) training.

Emergency Supplies

In addition to first aid supplies, your site will need other items in its emergency kits, sometimes called "crisis response boxes." These kits should be assembled in advance so they are available in a lockdown or evacuation situation.

Schools and houses of worship should have at least two kits in different locations (main office and elsewhere) and may have additional supply kits in individual classrooms or work areas.

Suggested Emergency Kit Contents

Administration or Main Office Supplies

- Clipboard or binder with:
    - Emergency operations plan
    - Quick reference guides to all emergency procedures
    - Reunification plan
    - Evacuation sites
    - A copy of the most recent security assessment
    - Site plan information, including:
        - Maps and photos
        - Building floor plan with utility shut-offs and detailed instructions on disablement
        - Bus routes and driver contact information
- Lists and contact information:
    - Emergency responders

- o Lists of all occupants, including staff, students or congregants, and volunteers
  - o Identification of persons with access or functional needs and a description of the need
  - o Attendance
  - o Current yearbook or photo sheets
  - o Personnel directory
- Rescue whistle
- Hat or brightly colored vest for visibility and leadership identification
- Leather work gloves
- Eye and hearing protection
- Battery-operated flashlight
- Emergency communication device
- First-aid kit with instructions
- Keys
- Release forms

Classroom, Nursery, Other Area Supplies

- Clipboard with lists of:
  - o All students, congregants, or children in area of responsibility
  - o Persons with access or functional needs and a description of the need
  - o Room leaders
- Rescue whistle
- Hat or brightly colored vest for visibility and leadership identification
- Pens and paper
- Age-appropriate activities
- First-aid kit with instructions
- Evacuation site maps
- Release forms

Emergency Procedures

Your plan should clearly spell out how the response actions described earlier in this lesson will be used to manage the situation until law enforcement arrives. Select the link below to access questions that can be used to guide the development process.

In addition to managing the initial crisis, your plan should indicate:

- What to do when law enforcement arrives.
- What to do after the situation is brought under control.

Key Questions for Response Protocols

In developing emergency response procedures, it is helpful to consider the following questions:

- What is the action?
- Who is responsible for the action?
- When should the action take place?
- How long should the action take and how much time is actually available?
- What has to happen before?
- What happens after?
- What resources are needed to perform the action?

When Law Enforcement Arrives

When law enforcement arrives, people at your site need to know what to expect and how to act to remain safe. The first officers to arrive will focus on stopping the assailant(s) as quickly as possible and will not stop to help injured persons. People at the site should remain calm, and follow officer instructions:

- Put items down.
- Raise their hands and spread their fingers.
- Keep hands visible at all times.
- Avoid making quick movements toward officers.
- Avoid pointing, screaming, or yelling.

After the Situation Is Under Control

Once an incident is under control, important steps still remain:

- Know in advance who will be responsible for communicating information about the incident and how that information will be shared with your community—both your immediate community and the one at large.
- Know how and where people will be cared for, protected from further injury and emotional trauma.
- Have a process to safely release people. The release of people to loved ones sometimes takes place before an incident has ended completely.

The next lesson provides more information on reunification and providing public information.

Putting It All Together

An immediate, appropriate response depends on having a plan with clearly articulated roles, responsibilities, and procedures. It also requires communicating those procedures in a way that enables personnel to use them in a moment of crisis.

With proper training and practice, the personnel at your site will be able to respond appropriately and quickly. In a later lesson, you will learn about communicating, training, and exercising the plan to ensure you are prepared.

Tip: Creating User-Friendly Procedures

In a crisis, no matter how much time was spent on planning, people are still likely to be surprised and confused. Decisions will need to be made within seconds, and those decisions will be made under stress. Procedures are most useful in these situations when they:

- Provide the right amount of information. (Too much detail can't be processed quickly.)
- Use clear, common language usable by diverse audiences.
- Are provided in user-friendly formats like posters, cards, placards, and flip-cards.
- Are posted prominently throughout the site, eating areas, class/meeting rooms, congregation areas, etc.
- Are produced in large enough type to be quickly and easily read.

Sample Procedures

Sample Evacuation Procedures

When implementing evacuation procedures:

Site lead:

- Public safety (911) shall be notified immediately when an evacuation of the site occurs.
- Determine evacuation routes based on location of the incident and types of emergency.
- Communicate the need to evacuate the building or a specific area of the building (utilizing onsite evacuation location inside the building) to the building occupants by activating the fire alarm or plain language via public address system or bullhorn.

- Communicate changes in evacuation routes based on location and types of emergency.
- Notify appropriate senior personnel that an evacuation has occurred.
- Designated staff assigned radios and/or cell phones should wear their lime-green vests.
- The Emergency Evacuation Kit and the Emergency Medical Bag should be moved outside with the evacuees.
- Monitor the situation and provide updates and additional instructions as needed.
- During inclement weather, consider requesting buses for sheltering students.
- Communicate when it is safe to re-enter the building or re-occupy a section of the building that was evacuated (i.e., bell system, radio transmission, public address system, or bull horn).

Staff:

- Exit the building using the designated emergency exit routes or as directed by the site lead. Emergency exit routes are diagramed on the site floor plan drawing posted near the light switch inside each room.
  - Use a secondary route if the primary route is blocked or hazardous.
- Exit routes will be selected and communicated by the site lead at the time of the emergency and the evacuation.
- Assist those with access and functional needs.
- Assigned staff or volunteers should wear the orange-colored vest located in the back pocket in each room.
- Do not lock doors when leaving.
- Do not stop for belongings.
- Take roster with you.
- Go to designated evacuation assembly area (minimum of 500 feet from building required in fire evacuation and 1,000 feet from building for bomb threat, 300 feet for chemical spill inside building, or other directed evacuations).
- When outside the building or onsite inside the building evacuation location:
  - Check for injuries.
  - Account for all people for whom you are responsible.
  - Immediately report any missing, extra, or injured people.
  - Continue to maintain control of those people for whom you are responsible.
- Wait for additional instructions.

When implementing offsite evacuation procedures:

Site lead:

- Public safety (911) should be notified immediately when an evacuation of a building occurs.
- Onsite evacuation procedures should be executed prior to initiating an offsite evacuation.
- Designated staff assigned radios and/or cell phones should wear their lime-green vests.
- The Emergency Evacuation Kit and the Emergency Medical Bag shall be moved outside the building with the evacuees.
- Determine if circumstances require people to be evacuated to an offsite location.
- Prior to initiation of an offsite evacuation, the site lead, program manager, or designee shall consult with and obtain authorization when necessary.
- Notify staff of the plan to evacuate to an offsite location.
- Notify the receiving site prior to initiation of the offsite movement.
- Make other notifications as necessary, communications, community outreach, transportation, etc.
- Announce evacuation.
  - Specify any changes in offsite evacuation routes based on location and types of emergency.
- Implement release procedures at the offsite location, if applicable.
- Document the release of any minors to an authorized family member or legal guardian.

Staff:

- Implement evacuation procedures for onsite evacuation location outside of the building.
- Follow direction of site lead concerning movement to offsite location.
- Remain with your assigned group while en route to the offsite location.
- Take attendance upon arriving at the offsite location.
- Check for injuries.
- Immediately report any missing, extra, or injured people.
- Continue to maintain control.
- Wait for additional instructions.

Adapted from: *Fairfax County (VA) Schools Crisis Management Workbook,* http://www.fcps.edu/emergencyplan/crisisresponse.shtml

Sample Emergency Lockdown Procedures

Site lead:

- Communicate the need to lockdown the building via the public address system.

o If you know the whereabouts of the assailant (e.g., outside the library or on the second floor, etc.), include this information in the lockdown announcement or any subsequent announcements; that way people can gauge whether they have an opportunity to evacuate versus lockdown. If individuals and groups are able to evacuate, they should move to the offsite evacuation location, if accessible. If not, they should choose a location as far as possible from the source of danger.
  o If known, relay the type of weapon the intruder is in possession of (firearm, knife, etc.).
- Direct all occupants to the nearest classroom or secured space occupied by staff members(s).
- Notify law enforcement (911) of the emergency and the need for immediate assistance.
- **DO NOT** attempt to lock exterior hallway doors that are unlocked.
- No one enters the school, except public safety personnel.

Lockdown Announcement – Class/Service in Progress
Attention, this is an emergency. At this time secure everyone in your rooms and take roll. If not in a room, report directly to the nearest room with a staff member.

Lockdown Announcement – Class/Service Change in Progress
Attention, this is an emergency. At this time secure everyone in a room and take roll. Everyone report directly to the nearest room with a staff member.

Lockdown Announcement – During Meal Periods
Attention, this is an emergency. At this time secure everyone in a room and take roll. Anyone in the eating area is to remain in the area and staff will secure the doors. Anyone outside of a room or eating area report directly to the nearest room with a staff member.

Staff

The following guidelines can be used by staff or designated others to determine if evacuation is a viable option versus lockdown:

- If you know the whereabouts of the violent intruder and you feel that you and those in your charge can safely evacuate the building and move to the student offsite evacuation location, if accessible, then do so. If not accessible, choose a location away from the source of danger.
  o Factors to consider in making the decision to evacuate versus lockdown:
    - Mobility: Is everyone able to move quickly or is their mobility limited due to access or functional needs?
    - Distance and/or concealment: Is there sufficient distance between you and the intruder to allow enough time to move

the group and reach safety and/or sufficient concealment along your evacuation route to move undetected?
- Type of weapon the intruder has in his or her possession: Knowing an intruder has a knife versus a firearm may affect your decision to lockdown or evacuate.

Implement lockdown procedures:

- Clear everyone from hallways into rooms.
- Assist those with access and functional needs.
- Close and lock all windows and doors; close window blinds, obscure door windows with paper.
- Block door with furniture, if appropriate.
- Turn lights off.
- Prepare a plan of action if the intruder gains entry (e.g., all-out assault on the intruder).
- Follow specified protocols if evacuation is initiated by law enforcement personnel.
- If a fire alarm has been activated, do not evacuate **UNLESS** fire or smoke is visible.
- Direct students to an area of the room, unobservable from outside and potential lines of fire.
- Stay away from all doors and windows.
- **BE QUIET!** Turn off the ringer on all cell phones.
- Move outside groups to primary or alternate offsite evacuation location.
- Persons in other buildings should remain inside the locked buildings.
- If you have evacuated the building, call 911 to report your location and situation.

Adapted from: *Fairfax County (VA) Schools Crisis Management Workbook,* http://www.fcps.edu/emergencyplan/crisisresponse.shtml

Sample Procedures for Reverse Evacuation and Preventive Lockdown

Preventive lockdown procedures are used to protect building occupants from potential dangers outside the building—e.g., police in pursuit of armed robbery suspect, or hostage/barricade situation near the school.

- Outside activities are cancelled and participants are moved inside.
- All exterior doors on buildings and trailers are secured.
- Occupants are free to move about inside the building/trailers.

Site lead:

- Communicate the need to secure the building (preventive lockdown) via the public address system and portable radio.

- No one is allowed outside of buildings.
- All building exterior doors are closed and locked.
- Those inside the building are free to move about within the building.
- Post staff at building main entrance to control visitor access, issue passes, and provide directions to reunification area, if applicable.
- If buses or other transportation are scheduled to arrive or depart from the site during the lockdown, advise them to remain offsite until resolved.
- When the threat has been mitigated, make announcement to return to normal operations.

Staff:

- Cancel outdoor activities and move participants inside the building.
- Close and lock perimeter doors.
- Do not allow anyone to exit the building unless directed by site lead.
- **DO NOT OPEN EXTERIOR DOORS.**

Adapted from: *Fairfax County (VA) Schools Crisis Management Workbook,*
http://www.fcps.edu/emergencyplan/crisisresponse.shtml

Sample Room Clear Procedures

Pre-event:

- Identify buddy rooms, and specific location in the building where people will be sent if a room clear is ordered.
- Maintain a list of the buddy rooms.
- Identify buddy rooms on a site map.

Event:

In case of the need to send people from a room or area to a safer location in the building, use the following procedures.

Staff member in room being cleared:

- Announce: Room clear, please go to [indicate buddy room].
- Direct people to leave in a calm, orderly manner.
- Notify the main office and briefly describe the situation and the response needed, such as 911 or first aid.
- Remain with the problem situation if it appears safe to do so.
- Stay calm.
- Take any extra precautions to keep yourself and others safe.

Staff member in buddy room:

- Notify main office of receiving people.
- Account for all people.

Adapted from: Lincoln County (OR) School District Emergency Procedures on video,
http://lincoln.k12.or.us/dept_programs/safety_videos.php

Sample Reverse Evacuation Procedures

In case of the need to send people from outside to a safer location in the building, use the following procedures.

Site lead:

- Announce: Reverse evacuation. Please follow reverse evacuation procedures.
- If other procedures are also to be implemented, such as a lockdown, announce those procedures also.
- When necessary use radios, megaphones, and runners (if safe) to contact staff outside.
- Make proper notifications, such as 911.

Staff Member:

- Instruct people to move quickly, but in a safe orderly fashion.
- Remain alert for possible threats while heading to the building and, when appropriate, adjust your route.
- When inside, follow instructions from site lead (for example, find the closest lockdown area).
- Remain calm and provide reassurance.
- Account for all people.

Remember: All staff members are empowered to implement a reverse evacuation when they deem it necessary.

Adapted from: Lincoln County (OR) School District Emergency Procedures on video,
http://lincoln.k12.or.us/dept_programs/safety_videos.php

Sample Procedures for Evacuation to Reunification Site

Pre-event

Site lead responsibilities:

- Organize the crisis team.

- Assign the crisis team tasks for:
    - Identifying buddy guidelines.
    - Conducting building evacuation.
    - Identifying relocation procedures.
    - Monitoring of relocation area.

Administrative/teacher/faculty responsibilities:

- Verify and maintain a list of people onsite, using rosters or other sign-in documents.
- Know the buddy guidelines.
- Know evacuation procedures to safe assembly area.

Event

Site lead responsibilities:

- Direct students, congregants, staff, and volunteers to evacuate the building to safe assembly areas.
- Identify safe evacuation procedures for people with access and functional needs.
- Meet with law enforcement and emergency responders.
- Account for all students, congregants, staff, and volunteers.
- Coordinate with law enforcement to direct emergency vehicles and other vehicles for transport to the relocation area.
- Identify a coordinator to assist loading of people on vehicles, and document vehicles and people on the vehicles.
- Direct the vehicles to the safe reunification site.
- Take emergency kits and information on students, congregants, staff, and volunteers.
- Stay at incident site—site lead or designee.
- Establish a check-in/check-out process at the reunification site. Crisis team members assist with check-in/check-out.
- Establish an area for students/congregants and a separate area for household members/loved ones.
- Establish a medical and counseling center at the reunification site. Crisis team members assist as needed.
- Have the reunification team members wear vests, badges, hats, and/or other indicators of their role.

Administrative/teacher/faculty responsibilities:

- Follow site lead directions.

- Move his or her group to the pre-designated assembly point and maintain order.
- Account for everyone once in the assembly area.
- Report anyone missing or injured.
- Check with buddy.
- Put group on vehicle to reunification site.
- Account for everyone once on vehicle.
- Maintain calm and order on vehicle.
- Proceed to the reunification site.

Adapted from: Evacuation Plan Pre-Event and Event Checklists (Orange County Schools), http://rems.ed.gov/docs/repository/00000723.pdf

Resources and Guidance

You can use the following resources to learn more about establishing response protocols.

- Readiness and Emergency Management for Schools, Technical Assistance Center, Helpful Hints:
    - Engaging Students in Emergency Management
    - Emergency "Go-Kits"
    - Steps for Developing a School Emergency Management Plan
    - Emergency Management Planning for Institutions of Higher Education
- Readiness and Emergency Management for Schools, Technical Assistance Center, Resource Repository
- Campus Safety
- Safe Havens International
- Mississippi Office of Homeland Security, Preparing for Worship Place Violence and Emergencies
- Denton (TX) Police Department, Violence Prevention Tips for a House of Worship
- DHS Active Shooter Preparedness
- IS-907, Active Shooter: What You Can Do

Lesson Summary

You should now understand the importance of creating response procedures for a secure and safe environment and the different situations and audiences these response procedures need to address.

The next lesson presents the considerations for returning to learning, or worship, and restoring the infrastructure of the facility as quickly as possible.

Lesson 5: After an Incident

After an Incident: Planning for Recovery

Mass casualty response planning is part of an all-hazards approach to planning. This lesson will describe planning considerations for managing the recovery process following a mass casualty incident.

After completing this lesson, you should be able to identify:

- The role of crisis recovery teams in recovery.
- Considerations for community recovery immediately following an incident.
- Promising practices for longer term community recovery.

Planning for Recovery

Mass casualty incidents often last just a few minutes while having a lasting effect on communities. And, the recovery process requires that the whole community join together.

The initial recovery involves a unity of effort between law enforcement to begin the investigative process and crisis recovery teams to begin the reunification and healing process.

Teams of staff, counselors, faith-based leaders, and others attend to the emotional needs of survivors and their loved ones.

Public information officers help ensure that family members and the community receive accurate information while protecting the privacy of those affected by the incident. In addition, these individuals help dispel rumors.

Crisis recovery teams consider other practical details such as how to handle the outpouring of donations from the local and extended community, and how best to manage memorials.

In this lesson you will learn how the recovery process helps provide emotional support and rebuilds a climate of safety and security.

Post-Incident Recovery

The goal of recovery is to successfully overcome the impacts—physical and emotional—of the incident and to return to the main mission of learning, or worship, as quickly as possible. After a mass casualty incident, the greatest focus will be on providing a caring and supportive environment and helping survivors recover emotionally. In addition, the recovery process needs to support law enforcement's investigative objectives.

In the beginning, the process may be intensive and stressful, with demands from many directions. It may be emotionally taxing, as situations involving fear, shock, and grief inevitably are. And it is likely to last for an extended period because healing takes time.

A recovery plan provides the foundation for uniting the whole community carrying out this process in a coordinated manner and for having the appropriate resources available when needed.

In the beginning, the process may be intensive and stressful, with demands from many directions. It may be emotionally taxing, as situations involving fear, shock, and grief inevitably are. And it is likely to last for an extended period because healing takes time.

A recovery plan provides the foundation for uniting the whole community carrying out this process in a coordinated manner and for having the appropriate resources available when needed.

Recovery Issues

Planning for recovery will help you identify issues and make decisions to guide the recovery process. For example, you may need to consider such questions as:

- How will reunification with families and loved ones be handled?
- What type of coordination will be needed with law enforcement?
- What, how, and when should we tell people about an incident?
- How will counseling resources be provided?
- Are critical incident stress management teams needed?
- How should survivors be encouraged to express their reactions?
- How will we handle public information?
- Should we turn to outside consultation for help? To whom?
- How soon should we return to regular routines?
- Should we plan commemorative activities?
- What is the best way to assist families and loved ones of victims and survivors?

Planning for Recovery

Planning in the following areas can help you answer these questions. In the sections that follow, we will explore some of the key considerations related to each area.

- Establishing Recovery Procedures
- Establishing Crisis Recovery Teams
- Preparing for the Return to Routine

Establishing Recovery Procedures

Recovery begins immediately after an incident and continues throughout the healing process and even as regular operations resume.

To facilitate this process, procedures should be developed for supporting key recovery functions, including:

- Reunification.
- Information management.
- Provision of counseling and support services.
- Planning for healing events and memorials.
- Managing donations.

Reunification

After a mass casualty incident it is important to quickly reunite survivors with their loved ones. Often, the best approach is to relocate survivors to a location away from the incident scene. Key planning considerations include:

- Site selection and security.
- Transportation logistics.
- Resources.
- Protocols for notification, information release, orderly check-in, check-out, record keeping, and release of minors to adults.

Reunification Tips

The reunification decision should be made quickly—within 5 to 10 minutes of the event. As soon as the media begins reporting an incident, it is natural for concerned individuals to rush to the scene unless given other guidance. Conducting reunification at the incident site has several disadvantages. It may:

- Hamper emergency response and crime scene investigation.
- Complicate an already emotionally charged situation.
- Expose family members to the media and onlookers.

Below are suggestions for reunification procedures.

- **Site selection and security:** Select a site that:
  - Is available at a moment's notice. Have a backup site.
  - Is safe—away from any damage and out of sight of assembly areas.
  - Can be secured and people entering the area be screened.
  - Has enough parking and enough safe entrances and exits to minimize congestion.
  - Is accessible by individuals with access and functional needs.
  - Has secure and safe facilities for individuals while they wait (e.g., shelter, restrooms, food).
  - Allows for limiting access by the media and the general public.
- **Transportation logistics:** Coordinate with:
  - Transportation officials to verify that everyone can be safely evacuated.
  - Security staff to identify ways to maintain control and limit access to the site.
  - Public safety personnel to coordinate traffic and parking support.
- **Resources:** Station key resources at the site, including:
  - Crisis recovery personnel, including law enforcement and security personnel.
  - Initial mental health personnel.
  - The emergency kit containing records and release forms and first aid supplies.
- **Protocols:**
  - Plan for immediate notification to loved ones through local media.
  - Do not publicly announce the location before an incident, to reduce the possibility of a secondary attack at the site.
  - Have procedures for the release of minors, such as photo identification.
  - Consider seeking help from local emergency management to manage the center.
  - Consider sharing evacuation and reunification portions of your emergency plan with parents/guardians in advance. Experience has shown that if parents/guardians are aware of the procedures before an event, they are less likely to go directly to an incident site.

The Need for Information

Mass casualty incidents are extraordinarily emotional events, and they leave intense emotions in their wake. The stress and uncertainty created by the incident tend to linger on, both in the survivors and witnesses to the event and in the community at large. When intense emotions can propel community members to action, effective messages from officials can help them make appropriate decisions.

After a mass casualty incident, people need clear, timely, and factual information to avoid relying on rumors. Great distress can make it hard for people to process information, so it is important to word messages simply, repeat them often, and provide regular updates.

Keeping Staff and Volunteers Informed

In an educational setting, teachers and staff carry much of the load in reestablishing a sense of security and providing support. In a religious setting, this role may be filled by faith-based leaders, volunteers, teachers, and others. Procedures should address training these individuals and keeping them well informed. Consider:

- How and when will you notify staff of an event?
- How will you provide them with more indepth information about the situation and their roles?
- How much information will you provide?
- How will you keep them updated?
- How will you obtain their input on improving the process and about their own need for assistance?

Ideas for Keeping Staff and Volunteers Informed

- Activate a notification process such as a calling tree or email/pager alerts to notify them of the event. Do this immediately after the event. Provide a script so the message does not degrade as it is passed from one person to the next. Advise them of the next day's morning meeting.
- Hold a morning meeting for all staff the first day after the incident, before the regular school or work day. This meeting may be used to:
    - Explain the incident in greater detail, including details that were not initially known.
    - Answer staff questions.
    - Introduce the crisis recovery team, crisis consultant if used, community resource people, and media and family liaisons.
    - Spell out the plan for the day.
    - Provide locations of a crisis center room, counseling rooms, and other resources.
    - Ensure everyone knows their role.
- Hold a similar meeting at the end of the day to review progress, answer questions, share insights, and set out plans for the next day.
- Keep staff updated with daily newsletters.
- Obtain a central contact from the law enforcement organizations who can answer questions and address concerns. Provide that information to staff members.

Fighting Rumors With Facts

In the absence of factual information, rumors inevitably fill the void. It is essential to get the facts out quickly to ensure an accurate message. In planning for communications, consider how you will be proactive in communicating the facts, deliver a positive message that you are attending to security, and keep updated information flowing.

Be sure to make information available in diverse, culturally appropriate, and age-specific formats to reach multiple audiences. And keep a careful balance between providing enough information to dispel rumors and protecting the privacy of victims and survivors.

Tips for Providing Information

- Develop templates in advance of incidents with prepared statements so that general information can be released quickly.
- Agree with partners to coordinate messages and to speak as one voice. Establish a schedule for the release of information and briefings.
- Write a letter to families and loved ones the first day after the incident about the incident, memorials, and available support.
- Issue updates as more information becomes available. Consider using a Web site to share updated information.
- Provide tip sheets for families/caregivers/loved ones on how to provide support. Examples of tip sheets are available from:
    - Federal Emergency Management Agency. (2004). *Helping Children Cope with Disaster*. http://www.fema.gov/pdf/library/children.pdf
    - National Association of School Psychologists. (2006). *Talking to Children About Violence: Tips for Parents and Teachers*. Retrieved from http://www.nasponline.org/resources/crisis_safety/talkingviolence.pdf
    - U.S. Department of Education. (n.d.). *Tips for Helping Students Recovering from Traumatic Events*. Retrieved from http://www2.ed.gov/parents/academic/help/recovering
    - U.S. Department of Health and Human Services. (2102, November). *Tips for Talking With and Helping Children and Youth After a Disaster or Traumatic Event: A Guide for Parents, Caregivers, and Teachers*. Retrieved from http://store.samhsa.gov/shin/content//SMA12-4732/SMA12-4732.pdf
- Conduct a community meeting where people can voice their concerns and be assured that safety issues are being addressed. Include law enforcement representatives to answer questions and address concerns.

Managing Media Involvement

Very soon after a mass casualty incident, the media will arrive at the scene. Managing the media can be a challenge—especially if individual reporters are insensitive to the needs of survivors. However, when managed effectively the media can also be an asset.

After any incident, it is important to speak with one voice and to manage the release of information without compromising the investigation. To accomplish these objectives, the Incident Commander should assign a Public Information Officer (PIO) to coordinate the release of information to families, community members, and the media. In a complex incident, there may be several PIOs representing different organizations. Coordination among the PIOs is important to avoid disseminating conflicting information.

Form mutually beneficial relationships:

- Cooperate with the media, but do not let them dictate.
- Remember, each reporter will seek a unique angle or perspective. Individual interviews can be good opportunities to get information out.
- Try to ensure that all reporters hear the same information.
- National and perhaps international media typically arrive. Do not forget the local media.

Plan what you will say:

- Convey a message of resilience, continued healing, and a return to normalcy.
- Be proactive about pitching story ideas to the media that promote hope and healing.
- Issue media advisories about memorial events open to the public, anniversary dates, fundraising or donations, etc.
- In preparing a media message, think about:
    - What are the facts? Clarify the situation.
    - What DO you know, and what do you NOT know?
    - What steps are you taking to address the situation?
    - Provide a "call to action" for members, or parents, or students.
    - Express empathy.
- Develop two or three key messages that are honest, consistent, responsive, and responsible. Strive to be positive and proactive.
- Never guess, speculate, or predict the future. Do not release information until you have verified its accuracy. Never go off the record. Avoid saying, "No comment."

Consider privacy issues:

- Consider privacy issues and release of victim and perpetrator names. What are the roles of law enforcement, schools, hospitals, and families in releasing names and conditions of victims?

- Have a carefully considered and crafted policy regarding release of staff, member, or student photos; yearbooks; congregational directories; and the like. Think about laws such as the Family Educational Rights and Privacy Act.

Manage media coverage of benchmark dates:

- The media will cover benchmark events, such as the first anniversary. Establish a media area where the media will set up cameras so as not to intrude on the ceremony. Create a perimeter for photographers and satellite trucks.
- Set guidelines on still and video cameras in the building.
- Develop a list of people willing to talk to the media.
- Decide if you will have a media pool (selected media representatives who share information) or allow all media to attend.
- If possible, meet with the media in advance to establish mutually beneficial guidelines.
- Ask the media to:
    - Refrain from replaying or reprinting images of the crisis. Showing disturbing pictures has the potential to re-traumatize victims.
    - Honor the victims while not glorifying the perpetrators.
    - Avoid memorizing suicides in order to discourage copycats.
    - Respect the privacy of those who do not want to be interviewed.
    - Consider a "no fly" zone over an outdoor memorial service.

Available training:

To learn more about public information, you may wish to take the following course. Additional training may be available through your State or local emergency management agency.

- IS-29: Public Information Officer Awareness
  http://training.fema.gov/EMIWeb/IS/courseOverview.aspx?code=IS-29

Providing Counseling and Support Services

In the wake of a traumatic incident, a significant part of the recovery effort will be devoted to providing counseling and support services to help with the process of emotional recovery. Research suggests that:

- People who have witnessed a traumatic event find comfort in returning to routine and being in the company of their peers and trusted adults, need to reestablish their sense of safety and security, and may have a need to talk about the experience.
- Early, brief, and focused intervention can reduce social and emotional distress.

- Some individuals have more difficulty coping and may require more indepth professional assistance for emotional recovery.

Referrals and Interventions

Based on the research findings and the principles of mental health triage, recovery plans should address:

- Engaging staff in initially assessing emotional needs.
- Identifying individuals who need mental health referrals.
- Providing limited interventions, such as group discussion, for those not in need of urgent mental health services.
- Identifying available services for families, loved ones, and community members who may want to seek assistance for their children or themselves.

Crisis recovery teams are instrumental in ensuring that appropriate interventions are provided. You will learn more about crisis recovery teams later in this lesson. Making sure that counselors and support service personnel are qualified and trustworthy is critical. Be sure to select and prescreen these resources in advance of an incident.

Psychological First Aid

Psychological first aid is a process that can be quickly learned and applied by educators to assist with emotional recovery. It involves five simple steps:

- **Listen**—Provide an opportunity to share experiences and express feelings.
- **Protect**—Protect individuals from further trauma and help reestablish feelings of physical and emotional safety.
- **Connect**—Help individuals reestablish supportive connections.
- **Model**—Demonstrate calm and optimistic behavior.
- **Teach**—Help individuals understand the normal range of stress reactions.

Support for Staff and Volunteers

Members of the crisis recovery team can easily become overwhelmed by dealing with intensely emotional topics over a long period. It is important to ensure that those who are providing psychological first aid are also supported. Possible measures include:

- Critical incident stress debriefings.

- Arranging for substitutes or time off when needed.
- Mechanisms that enable staff to provide support for one another during a crisis.
- Openly communicating opportunities for support and assistance.
- Recognizing the efforts being made.

Planning Healing Events and Memorials

Plans should be established regarding how victims will be memorialized. Examples of issues that may be addressed include:

- Guidelines regarding planned memorials and activities to honor victims.
- How spontaneous memorials on the premises will be addressed.
- Policies related to attendance at funerals and other memorial events.
- Identifying the appropriate time and way to signal closure of the mourning period.
- Including the whole community in planning memorials and other key events.

Lesson Learned

Lesson Learned: Proceed With Caution When Planning Memorials and Tributes for Victim(s)

Research has shown that constructing or conducting memorials may result in recurring trauma and may require ongoing funding for maintenance. When considering memorials or tributes the community must consider the cultural norms of the community, family preferences, and the long-term implications for how the memorial will be viewed by students and the community 5, 10, or 15 years after the incident. Memorials should never interfere with the teaching and learning environment.

Managing Donations

Often after a tragedy, people from across the country, and even the world, want to express their condolences through cards, memorabilia, gifts, and cash donations. These donations pressure an organization into making quick decisions about handling the gifts. Having a plan in place to manage donations can help relieve this pressure. Your local or State government may have a donations management plan and may be available to assist.

Consider:

- Establishing outreach messages to discourage inappropriate donations.
- Determining how to advise interested parties about preferred forms of donation.
- Setting up procedures for accountability and receipt of funds and materials.

- Establishing managing and disseminating donations received.

Donations Management: One Town's Experience

Following the 2012 tragedy at Sandy Hook Elementary School in Newtown, CT, volunteers struggled to manage the overwhelming flow of donations. The town received enough teddy bears to give two to every community member. The town established a task force of more than 800 volunteers to sort the gifts, open mail, and answer the thousands of emails and phone calls offering assistance.

After meeting with town officials, the Red Cross, and other stakeholders, a donations coordinator was identified. Volunteers started working in their living rooms with a couple of cellphones and their own laptop computers.

Next, a local businessperson offered office space and other companies donated computers, Wi-Fi, phones, and other equipment and set up a call center. The Newtown Volunteer Task Force established a Web site, a Facebook page, a Twitter account, and a toll-free telephone number.

The town established a partnership with Adventist Community Services, a faith-based group that has done similar work after hurricanes and other natural disasters. This group has warehouse facilities and experience collecting, organizing and distributing donated goods.

Establishing Crisis Recovery Teams

Crisis recovery teams manage the impact of serious incidents. A crisis recovery team can help in the healing process by:

- **Planning for immediate postincident actions**—Identifying and contacting any at-risk survivors, holding meetings with family or the community, and updating the plan.
- **Establishing casualty and fatality process**—Determining who tells loved ones about casualties and fatalities.
- **Reducing fear**—Helping to restore confidence in the safety of the environment by discussing security measures and addressing fears that an incident may occur again.
- **Facilitating grieving**—Formulating a policy on funerals and other memorials, helping plan incident- and age-appropriate activities, and obtaining as needed the services of trained counselors and other experts from the community.
- **Supporting loved ones**—Answering questions about the incident and the response, and offering advice on addressing children's needs.

- **Promoting the primary mission**—Promoting the mission of the organization (education or worship) by supporting a return to regular schedules and calling in substitute personnel as needed.

Community responders may have resources available to help staff recovery teams.

Crisis Recovery Team Members

Crisis recovery teams should include counselors and others who are:

- Trained to handle emotional response issues.
- Able and authorized to make decisions.
- Respected within the organization and the community.
- Sensitive to student/member, staff, and community needs.
- Calm and able to make decisions in stressful situations.

Qualified mental health professionals in the community that can assist during recovery should be identified.

Tips for Organizing Crisis Teams

- Consider including:
    - Organization leaders—people with authority to make decisions in the time of crisis.
    - Staff—those who have day-to-day contact with survivors, such as teachers, counselors, coaches, faith-based leaders, or others.
    - Key personnel—Individuals who have expertise in aspects of recovery operations, such as communications systems, information management, or crowd control.
    - Law enforcement personnel—those who will conduct the investigation and interact with staff, leaders, survivors, and the community.
- If an incident occurs, it will be important to have professionals in the community who are able to respond quickly and who will be committed to the effort over time.
- Contact outside resources ahead of time to determine their availability and willingness to help by:
    - Being available to talk with individuals needing support or counseling.
    - Seeing professionally any individuals who are referred by the school.
- Once a support program has been set in motion, it is important to have continuity. Clarify understandings with key resources by establishing Memoranda of Understanding.
- Some organizations use a crisis consultant to help develop, review, and implement crisis plans. Sometimes consultants are able to be more objective than staff because they are not emotionally tied to the victims.

Crisis Recovery Team Responsibilities

The crisis recovery team should identify responsibilities for coordinating various aspects of recovery. Examples of key functions requiring coordination include:

- **Team Oversight**
  - **Crisis team chair**—Convenes scheduled and emergency team meetings, oversees both broad and specific team functions, ensures that the required resources are available to each team member for assigned duties, and communicates with the district-level team. Is often an administrator or designee.
  - **Assistant chair**—Assists the crisis team chair with all functions and substitutes for the chair in the chair's absence.
- **Incident crowd management**—In collaboration with law enforcement and first responders, develops and implements plans for crowd management and movement during crises, including any required evacuation plans and security measures. Crowd management plans must anticipate many scenarios, including the need to cordon off areas to preserve physical evidence or to manage increased vehicular and pedestrian traffic. Because of the possibility of actual threats to physical safety, crowd management plans must provide for safe and organized movement in a way that minimizes the risk of harm under various threats, such as sniper fire.
- **Staff notification coordinator**—Establishes, coordinates, and initiates the telephone tree to contact the crisis team and general staff, including itinerant, part-time, and paraprofessional staff. Also establishes a plan to rapidly disseminate relevant information to all staff during regular hours.
- **Communications coordinator**—Conducts all direct in-house communications, screens incoming calls, and maintains a log of telephone calls related to the crisis event. Helps the staff notification coordinator develop a notification protocol for a crisis event that occurs during the day.
- **Reunification coordinator**—Establishes the reunification center/area and manages the reunification process.
- **Public information officer**—Works through the Incident Command public information officer to deliver a single, coordinated message to the public. Prepares statements to disseminate to staff, students/members, families and loved ones, and the community. Maintains ongoing contact with law enforcement, emergency services, hospital representatives, and others to keep information current. Handles all media requests for information and responds through appropriate channels.
- **Coordinator of counseling**—Develops mechanisms for ongoing training of crisis team members and other staff and identifies and establishes liaisons with community resources for counseling. At the time of a crisis, determines the extent of counseling services needed, mobilizes community resources, and oversees the

mental health services provided to individuals. Must have appropriate counseling and mental health skills and experience.

Preparation and Training

In preparation for activation in a crisis, consider how team members will be trained in appropriate intervention techniques.

For example, local counselors may be able to train your staff and volunteers to make an initial assessment of the emotional needs of survivors and identify those who need additional services.

Training should focus on how crisis interventions can be applied in your particular setting and with your population.

Training Resources

Training that takes relatively little time is available through various sources. The following are examples:

- **The U.S. Department of Education** has information on an early intervention approach that staff can learn in as little as an hour.

  U.S. Department of Education. (2008). Psychological First Aid (PFA) for Students and Teachers: Listen, Protect, Connect—Model & Teach. *Helpful Hints for School Emergency Management. 3,3*. Retrieved from http://rems.ed.gov/docs/HH_Vol3Issue3.pdf

- **The National Organization for Victim Assistance** offers resources and training in community crisis response. NOVA's basic course covers techniques and protocols for providing crisis intervention to traumatized people. It focuses on the fundamentals of crisis and trauma, and how to adapt the basic techniques to individuals and groups.

  National Organization for Victim Assistance. (2012). *NOVA Training and Credentialing.*
  http://www.trynova.org/wp-content/uploads/2012/07/CRTTrainingBrochure.pdf

- **International Critical Incident Stress Foundation, Inc.** provides education, training, consultation, and support services in comprehensive crisis intervention and disaster behavioral health services to the emergency response professions, other organizations, and communities worldwide. http://www.icisf.org

Preparing for the Return to Routine

Establishing a routine and striving to achieve a "new normal" can help those impacted by an incident to recover. While things will never be quite the same, they will come to realize a new equilibrium can be achieved. During this phase:

- Work toward restoring the academic or worship environment.
- Continue mental health support.
- Regularly communicate with families and loved ones.
- Meet as needed with key stakeholders to identify questions, quell rumors, and provide accurate and timely information.
- Maintain structure and stability. Routine is good!

Resources

You can use the following resources to learn more about planning for recovery.

Online Resources:

- Helping Children Cope with Disaster.
- National Association of School Psychologists. Tips for crisis and safety, helping children cope, and related topics.
- National Education Association Health Information Network. School crisis resources.
- National Organization for Victim Assistance. Information on crisis response: Training and Credentialing.
- Practical Information on Crisis Planning: A Guide for Schools and Communities.
- Psychological First Aid (PFA) for Students and Teachers.
- Tips for Helping Students Recovering from Traumatic Events.
- Tips for Talking With and Helping Children and Youth Cope After a Disaster or Traumatic Event: A Guide for Parents, Caregivers, and Teachers.

Training:

- FEMA IS-29: Public Information Officer Awareness
- International Critical Incident Stress Foundation (ICISF): Crisis intervention training.

Lesson Summary

You should now understand planning considerations for managing the recovery process following a mass casualty incident.

The next lesson presents approaches for staying prepared through communicating and exercising your plan.

Lesson 6: Staying Prepared

Staying Prepared: Communicating and Exercising the Plan

After completing this lesson, you should be able to identify:

- Key factors in compiling the plan and getting approval.
- Key considerations for communicating the plan.
- Characteristics of an effective training and exercise program.
- The importance of taking corrective actions and updating the plan.

Staying Prepared

During the planning process, community partners consider what might happen before, during, and after an incident. They review all available information, including prior events, lessons learned, stakeholder concerns, legal requirements, vulnerabilities, and other information.

The team considers a range of options for assessing and mitigating vulnerabilities, responding to an incident, and recovering from an incident and selects the strategies that will be most effective in helping avert danger or minimize consequences.

After taking the time needed to assess and strategize, the team is ready to record these decisions and procedures in the planning document.

It is important to get buy-in and approval of the plan and to train others to implement the plan. After informing others about the plan, the next critical step is to conduct periodic drills and other exercises with students, congregation members, staff, volunteers, and community responders.

Staying prepared is a continuous process—not just a one-time planning effort or single drill. Preparedness requires a commitment to keeping the plan updated, practicing the procedures, and making improvements based on lessons learned.

Being Prepared: Success Stories

Lockdown drills pay off

In October 2010 at Kelly Elementary School in Carlsbad, CA, the lockdown drills paid off at lunch, when a gunman walked onto the campus and began to shoot at the students outside. The staff responded as practiced and safely ushered the students inside and locked down the building in 3 minutes. Although two students were injured, had the staff not been prepared, it could have been much worse.

Yesterday 'it worked'

In April 2010 at a middle school in Hastings, MN, a boy pulled a loaded gun out in class. His teacher convinced him to leave before anyone was harmed. Immediately, the office was alerted, the school locked down, and 911 called. As the boy walked the halls, he found the rooms locked. Police arrived and the boy was placed in custody. The police chief attributed the quick and effective response to the school having conducted safety drills saying, "…yesterday was a good example of 'it worked.'"

Staying Prepared

Staying prepared involves understanding your vulnerabilities and having a plan for before, during, and after an incident. It also requires communication, training, exercising, and plan maintenance to ensure that all participants remain ready to implement the plan.

This lesson will present an overview of strategies for staying prepared that are suggested by experienced emergency management professionals. Select the link below to view key research sources for this lesson.

Communicating the Plan

Turning ideas into a workable plan requires communication. Everyone who will take part in implementing the plan needs to understand what is supposed to happen, what actions they are responsible for, and how their roles fit into the overall scheme.

The first step in creating this shared awareness is to develop a written plan document that can be shared among the various stakeholders.

Developing the Plan Document

Your plan (or annex if an all-hazards emergency plan already exists) doesn't necessarily have to be complex or elaborate as long as it is:

Adequate—An adequate plan:

- Identifies critical tasks.
- Is based on valid and reasonable assumptions.
- Complies with guidance.

Feasible—A feasible plan:

- Can be accomplished with available resources.
- Identifies where and how needed outside resources will be obtained.

Acceptable—A plan is acceptable if it:

- Thoroughly addresses the identified threat situation.
- Complies with legal requirements and is consistent with any regulations that apply.
- Is compatible with local emergency plans.

Complete—A plan is considered complete if it:

- Includes all the tasks to be accomplished.
- Addresses individuals with functional and access needs.
- Provides a complete picture of what should happen, when, and at whose direction.
- Strikes a balance between providing sufficient guidance for carrying out common tasks, and avoiding too much detail.

Usable—An easy-to-use plan is one that:

- Uses simple, clear language, avoids jargon, and minimizes the use of abbreviations.
- Uses short sentences and the active voice. (Qualifiers and vague wording only add to confusion.)
- Summarizes important information with checklists and visual aids, such as maps and flowcharts.
- Can be used by all audiences, including those with access and functional needs.

Organizing and Formatting the Plan

A plan or annex can be organized in various ways. Be sure to format the plan for ease of use and present its contents so that its readers can quickly find solutions and options.

Checklist for Plan Organization and Format

- ☐ **Organization**
  - ☐ Can users find what they need?
  - ☐ Is all the information relevant?
  - ☐ Is the plan formatted clearly?
  - ☐ Is its content presented clearly?
- ☐ **Sequence**
  - ☐ Can users understand the rationale for the sequencing?
  - ☐ Are users able to scan for information they need?
- ☐ **Consistency**
  - ☐ Does each section use the same logical progression, or do users have to reorient themselves?
- ☐ **Adaptability and compatibility**
  - ☐ Is the information easy to use during unanticipated situations?
  - ☐ Can the information be applied or adapted to effectively respond to each unique situation?
  - ☐ Does the format promote or hinder coordination with local response agencies and personnel?

Guidance for Plan Development

You can learn more about organizing and writing a plan or annex from the following source:

- Comprehensive Preparedness Guide (CPG) 101: Developing and Maintaining Emergency Operations Plans

Schools

- **Sample School Emergency Operations Plan.** FEMA, March 2011. http://www.training.fema.gov/EMIWeb/emischool/EL361Toolkit/assets/SamplePlan.pdf
- **Sample Childcare Emergency Operations Plan.** FEMA, November 2011. http://training.fema.gov/EMIWeb/IS/IS36Materials/Handouts%20-Sample%20Plans/EOP_Sample.pdf

- **Sample Campus EOP.** Texas School Safety Center (Texas State University-San Marcos), 2010.
  http://www.txssc.txstate.edu/K12/eop
- **Sample District EOP.** Texas School Safety Center (Texas State University-San Marcos), 2010.
  http://www.txssc.txstate.edu/K12/eop
- **School Emergency Response Plan Annex for Crisis Response.** Illinois State Board of Education (no date). Access by going to http://www.isbe.net/safety/guide.htm, which links to School Emergency and Crisis Response Plan Template. From there, select III. K. Planned Responses/Teacher Action Guides -- SECURE MATERIALS to access the annex.

Institutions of Higher Education

- **Model Campus Emergency Response Plans.** National Association of College and University Business Officers.
  http://www.nacubo.org/Business_and_Policy_Areas/Risk_Management/Campus_Security/
  Emergency_Preparedness.htm
- **TAMU Emergency Operations Plan Annex V – Acts of Violence.** Texas A&M University, 2012.
  http://www.tamu.edu/emergency/documents/AnnexV.pdf
- **Plan Annex for Active Shooter.** Rutgers University, 2012.
  http://halflife.rutgers.edu/eap/eap.html

Houses of Worship

- **Emergency Plan Template for Faith Based Organizations.** Missouri Faith-Based Homeland Security Initiative, (no date).
  http://www.dmreligious.org/userdocs/knowledgecenter/
  Faith_Based_Emergency_Plan_Template_5-15-09.pdf
- **Emergency Action Plan for First Presbyterian Church.** (Waunakee, WI), September 9, 2011.
  http://www.myfpc.org/storage/building-and-grounds/
  FPC%20Emergency%20Action%20Plan%2009192011.pdf

Getting Buy-In for the Plan

After the team assembles the plan, it is important to get acceptance and commitment from key stakeholders, including:

- Those in your organization who will have a role in implementing the plan.
- Community partners, including law enforcement and first responders.
- Leadership in your organization with approval authority.

Commitment to the plan often results from using a collaborative planning process. It begins with the partnerships formed for planning and builds as the team works together to identify and develop strategies.

Tips for Getting Buy-In

- During the planning process, stress the benefit each partner gains from providing input to the plan. Their planning contributions will result in a plan that better reflects their own perspective.
- In presenting the plan, emphasize the importance of the plan for keeping people safe.
- Seek the widest acceptance possible for the plan. Invite feedback from both the personnel in your organization and from the broader community.
- Include agencies with emergency or homeland security responsibilities in order to collect suggestions for improvements to the plan.
- Remember to include support staff and trained volunteers, who play an important role in maintaining a secure and safe environment.
- Have each group carefully review the portion of the plan they are responsible for, and solicit their feedback.

Getting the Plan Approved

Most organizations will want to present the plan to the appropriate individuals for review, approval, and dissemination.

Placing a promulgation document in the front of the plan gives authority and responsibility to organization personnel to perform their tasks. A promulgation document:

- Allows the leadership to affirm their support for emergency management.
- Outlines the responsibilities of tasked organizations with regard to preparing and maintaining the plan.
- Conveys the commitment of those organizations to carrying out the training, exercises, and plan maintenance needed to support the plan.

Sharing the Plan With the Whole Community

Emergency preparedness is a community endeavor. Consider sharing the plan with a variety of stakeholders, which may include faculty, staff, faith-based leaders, trained volunteers, students and their households, members of the community, and the media.

For security reasons, the full details of the master plan are typically not made public. However, all stakeholders should know that a complete plan exists and should become familiar with any part of it that involves their participation.

There are many simple ways to communicate plan elements, from pamphlets to Web sites.

Tips for Sharing the Plan

- Conduct orientation meetings to explain why and how the plan was developed and provide an overview of the plan's contents. Include administrators, law enforcement, other community partners, and public information as presenters. Invite the media.
- Post critical information, such as evacuation procedures and routes, in easily visible locations within the facility.
- Provide information in bulletins and newsletters.
- Create pamphlets that can be sent home with students or members of the congregation.
- Produce pocket guides or wallet-sized cards with procedure reminders.
- Create refrigerator magnets for lounges, residence halls, offices, and households.
- Put publicly viewable parts of the plan on your Web site.

Providing Training

For a plan to serve its intended purpose, it needs to become part of the culture, not just a document on the shelf. Training should be provided to:

- Develop awareness of the plan.
- Underscore the importance of preparedness.
- Prepare personnel to carry out the planned procedures effectively.

Training may be given in the form of orientations, briefings, and seminars.

Simple Ideas for Providing Training

- Review safety and security procedures with ALL personnel, including:
    - Administrators, faculty, and staff.
    - Trained volunteers.
    - Janitorial, maintenance, transportation, food service, and other support personnel.
    - School Resource Officer (SRO) or guards/security staff (if any).
    - Public information officer/spokesperson.
    - Other involved personnel.

- Provide training for greeters and ushers. They play a key role in identifying potentially hazardous situations and initiating protective measures.
- Incorporate training into ongoing regular activities to keep people refreshed in how to implement procedures in a crisis.

  As an example, take 5 to 10 minutes at every meeting of faculty, staff, or volunteers to present a section of your plan and review the procedures. Allow ample time for discussion and questions to ensure that everyone is familiar with the responses. This interaction is great for newcomers and begins to promote a culture of safety, security, and preparedness.

  Look for similar opportunities that are appropriate for your situation.

- Give orientations for specific audiences, and invite emergency responders to attend and answer questions.
- Schedule brief presentations for students on specific procedures during homeroom, faith-based classes, youth group meetings, or other student activities. Follow the presentation with group discussion.

Exercising the Plan

In any endeavor, the ability to perform effectively comes from practice. The more you practice procedures laid out in the plan, the better you will be able to respond effectively if the need arises.

Exercises are a means to train, assess, practice, and improve performance in a safe environment.

Snapshot: According to a 2010 survey by the U.S. Department of Education, 84 percent of public schools had a written response plan for a shooting incident but only 52 percent had drilled their students on the plan in the past year. Providing more practice will help you stay better prepared.

Exercise Fundamentals

Local emergency management, first responders, and other relevant community partners should participate in the planning and conduct of exercises. When partners work together, exercises provide opportunities for:

- Testing and validating plans, policies or procedures, training, equipment, and interagency agreements.
- Clarifying roles and responsibilities.
- Improving individual performance.
- Identifying gaps in resources, planning, or assumptions.
- Most importantly, identifying opportunities to improve.

Types of Exercises

Several different types of exercises can be used to enhance your preparedness for potential mass casualty incidents. Exercises fall into the following two types:

Discussion-Based	Operations-Based
<ul><li>Seminars</li><li>Workshops</li><li>Tabletop exercises</li><li>Games</li></ul>	<ul><li>Drills</li><li>Functional exercises</li><li>Full-Scale exercises</li></ul>

Discussion-Based Exercises

Discussion-based exercises include seminars, workshops, tabletop exercises, and games. These types of exercises can be used to familiarize players with, or develop new, plans, policies, agreements, and procedures. Discussion-based exercises focus on strategic, policy-oriented issues. Facilitators and/or presenters usually lead the discussion, keeping participants on track towards meeting exercise objectives.

Seminars

Seminars generally orient participants to, or provide an overview of, authorities, strategies, plans, policies, procedures, protocols, resources, concepts, and ideas. They can be valuable for entities that are developing or making major changes to existing plans or procedures. Seminars can be similarly helpful when attempting to assess or gain awareness of the capabilities of interagency or inter-jurisdictional operations.

Workshops

Although similar to seminars, workshops differ in two important aspects: participant interaction is increased, and the focus is placed on achieving or building a product. Effective workshops entail the broadest attendance by relevant stakeholders. Products produced from a workshop can include new standard operating procedures, emergency operations plans, continuity of operations plans, or mutual aid agreements. To be effective, workshops should have clearly defined objectives, products, or goals, and should focus on a specific issue.

Tabletop Exercises

A tabletop exercise is intended to generate discussion of various issues regarding a hypothetical, simulated emergency. Tabletops can be used to enhance general awareness, validate plans and procedures, rehearse concepts, and/or assess the types of systems needed to guide the prevention of, protection from, mitigation of, response to, and recovery from a defined incident. Generally, tabletops are aimed at facilitating conceptual understanding, identifying strengths and areas for improvement, and/or achieving changes in perceptions.

During a tabletop, players are encouraged to discuss issues in depth, collaboratively examining areas of concern and solving problems. The effectiveness of a tabletop exercise is derived from the energetic involvement of participants and their assessment of recommended revisions to current policies, procedures, and plans.

Tabletops can range from basic to complex.

- In a basic tabletop (such as a Facilitated Discussion), the scenario is presented and remains constant—it describes an emergency and brings discussion participants up to the simulated present time. Players apply their knowledge and skills to a list of problems presented by the facilitator; problems are discussed as a group; and resolution is reached and documented for later analysis.
- In a more advanced tabletop, play advances as players receive pre-scripted messages that alter the original scenario. A facilitator usually introduces problems one at a time in the form of a written message, simulated telephone call, videotape, or other means. Players discuss the issues raised by each problem, referencing established authorities, plans, and procedures for guidance. Player decisions are incorporated as the scenario continues to unfold.

Games

A game is a simulation of operations that often involves two or more teams, usually in a competitive environment, using rules, data, and procedures designed to depict an actual or hypothetical situation. Games explore the consequences of player decisions and actions. They are useful tools for validating plans and procedures or evaluating resource requirements.

During game play, decisionmaking may be either slow and deliberate or rapid and more stressful, depending on the exercise design and objectives. The open, decision-based format of a game can incorporate "what if" questions that expand exercise benefits. Depending on the game's design, the consequences of player actions can be either pre-scripted or decided dynamically. Identifying critical decision-making points is a major factor in the success of evaluating a game.

Operations-Based Exercises

Operations-based exercises include drills, functional exercises, and full-scale exercises. These exercises can be used to validate plans, policies, agreements, and procedures; clarify roles and responsibilities; and identify resource gaps. Operations-based exercises are characterized by actual reaction to an exercise scenario, such as initiating communications or mobilizing personnel and resources.

Drills

A drill is a coordinated, supervised activity usually employed to validate a specific function or capability in a single agency or organization. Drills are commonly used to provide training on new equipment, validate procedures, or practice and maintain current skills. For example, drills may be appropriate for practicing evacuation procedures.

Drills can also be used to determine if plans can be executed as designed, to assess whether more training is required, or to reinforce best practices. A drill is useful as a stand-alone tool, but a series of drills can be used to prepare several organizations to collaborate in a full-scale exercise.

For every drill, clearly defined plans, procedures, and protocols need to be in place. Personnel need to be familiar with those plans and trained in the processes and procedures to be drilled.

Functional Exercises

Functional exercises are designed to validate and evaluate capabilities, multiple functions and/or sub-functions, or interdependent groups of functions. Functional exercises are typically focused on exercising plans, policies, procedures, and staff members involved in management, direction, command, and control functions.

In functional exercises, events are projected through an exercise scenario with event updates that drive activity typically at the management level. A functional exercise is conducted in a realistic, real-time environment; however, movement of personnel and equipment is usually simulated.

Functional exercise controllers typically use a Master Scenario Events List to ensure participant activity remains within predefined boundaries and ensure exercise objectives are accomplished. Simulators in a Simulation Cell can inject scenario elements to simulate real events.

Full-Scale Exercises

Full-scale exercises are typically the most complex and resource-intensive type of exercise. They involve multiple agencies, organizations, and jurisdictions and validate many facets of preparedness. Full-scale exercises often include many players operating under cooperative systems such as the Incident Command System (ICS) or Unified Command.

In a full-scale exercises, events are projected through an exercise scenario with event updates that drive activity at the operational level. Full-scale exercises are usually conducted in a real-time, stressful environment that is intended to mirror a real incident. Personnel and resources may be mobilized and deployed to the scene, where actions are performed as if a real incident had occurred. The full-scale exercise simulates reality by presenting complex and realistic problems that require critical thinking, rapid problem solving, and effective responses by trained personnel.

The level of support needed to conduct a full-scale exercise is greater than that needed for other types of exercises. The exercise site is usually large, and site logistics require close monitoring. Safety issues, particularly regarding the use of props and special effects, must be monitored. Throughout the duration of the exercise, many activities occur simultaneously.

Homeland Security Exercise and Evaluation Program (HSEEP)

The Homeland Security Exercise and Evaluation Program (HSEEP) provides a set of guiding principles for exercise programs, as well as a common approach to exercise program management, design and development, conduct, evaluation, and improvement planning.

Select this link to access information about HSEEP.
https://hseep.dhs.gov/support/HSEEP_Revision_Apr13_Final.pdf

Planning Exercises

When planning drills and other exercises, be sure you know your objective—what specific areas of your plan are to be tested:

- What function is to be tested?
- What personnel and resources are to be tested?
- What type of emergency will be addressed?
- What location will be used for the testing?
- What type of drill(s) will be used for testing?

Practicing From the Ground Up

It is important to create a progressive exercise program, beginning with simple exercises (e.g., simple tabletops and drills) and gradually introducing increasingly complex exercises that build upon the previous ones.

When conducting any exercise:

- Communicate information in advance. Doing so contributes to security awareness and avoids raising concern.
- Exercise under different conditions (e.g., classes/services in session, transition between classes/services, normal operations, special events).
- Debrief after each exercise and develop an after-action report and improvement plan.

Using Drills

Drills:

- Are an important way to practice a specific function, such as performing a reverse evacuation.
- Allow staff and trained volunteers to practice implementing the procedures and accounting for people under their supervision.
- Allow facility occupants (students, congregants, or others) to practice following procedures and instructions.

Preparing for Drills

Drills will be most successful when you lay the proper groundwork:

- Conduct a stakeholder meeting to confirm responsibilities of all entities.
- Train all participants in the procedures.

- Coordinate with security personnel and law enforcement—invite them to participate or observe.
- Check all communication systems relating to emergency notification.
- Conduct the drill first with staff and trained volunteers.
- Then conduct the drill with staff, trained volunteers, and all facility occupants.

Communications Drills

Communications drills are used to review and test communications protocols, including:

- **External communications:** Between different groups (e.g., your facility and various response agencies or community groups).
- **Internal communications:** Among personnel within your facility, such as between main office and individual rooms or groups that are outside the building.
- **Vertical communications:** Between your facility and your organizational hierarchy.

These types of drills can verify communications before conducting response action drills.

Response Drills

Response drills provide practice in specific emergency actions that may be required during a crisis. They can be facility-wide operations or initiated by staff with a subset of the population. Combination drills can also be created by combining response actions in a single drill. Examples of response drills include:

- Evacuation drills
- Lockdown drills
- Reverse evacuation drills
- Room clear drills

Drill Planning Checklist

Exercise Planning Team
Create a timeline for the drill.
Identify planning team members: site personnel, emergency responders, and community members.
Assign responsibilities to team members.
Design and Develop Drill
Identify type of drill.

| Identify where the drill will take place. |
| Identify who will participate in the drill. |
| Identify actions, procedures, and protocols that will be drilled. |

Prior to the Drill

| Be sure the procedures call for use of simple language to make announcements (lockdown, evacuation, reverse evacuation, room clear). |
| Review safety and security procedures with all staff, volunteers, members, and students. |
| Review each individual's emergency responsibilities. |
| Make proper notification of the plan to conduct a drill (parents, guardians, other). |
| Have an all clear procedure identified to end the drill. |
| Review and test communication protocols:

• Between different groups (site personnel, medical, law enforcement)
• Among site personnel
• With groups outside the building
• From rooms to the main office
• With other sites
• With parents/guardians |

During the Drill

| Determine if the emergency alert/announcement was clearly communicated and understood throughout the building. |
| Determine if the procedures and protocols were properly followed. |
| Identify if there was a method for room staff/volunteers to communicate with the main office. |
| Identify if the procedures for hallways, bathroom, and open areas were followed. |
| Identify if the procedures for individuals outside were followed. |

After the Drill

| Conduct a debriefing session with key partners to discuss lessons learned and measures for improvement. |
| Identify/discuss:

• How long the drill took
• What worked well
• What needs to be improved
• Other people needed for the drill team
• Emergency response time if this were not a drill |

	• Next steps
	Prepare an after-action report with observations of and recommendations for the drill.
Improvement Plan	
	Review and update plans and procedures per the after-action report.

Adapted from: State of New Jersey Department of Education School Security Drill Checklist, http://www.state.nj.us/education/schools/security/drill/SchoolSecurit%20DrillChecklist.pdf

Evacuation Drill Procedures

Before the Drill	
Assign each room or area a designated evacuation route and an alternate route.	Staff, volunteers, members, and students should be familiar with the evacuation routes. Primary and alternate routes should be identified.
Evacuation instructions should be posted in each room or area.	Posters with evacuation diagrams and instructions should be posted in each room or area.
Unique warnings	Emergency warnings should be clearly distinguishable from each other.
Ensure drill alarm systems are in working order.	All alarm systems should be kept in working order at all times.
Plan for alternate warning procedure and evacuation routes.	
Alert any necessary personnel in advance of the drill.	It may be necessary to notify food service personnel or other staff in advance of the drill.
Provide law enforcement and fire departments with the building floor plan, plans, and procedures.	
Assign responsibilities.	All staff and volunteers should be assigned responsibilities. A staff member or volunteer should evaluate conditions of the assembly area(s) before the evacuation.

Day of the Drill	
Notify 911 dispatchers of the drill.	Also provide notification when the drill is complete.
Issue evacuation order.	
Turn off computer monitors and other educational aids, where applicable.	
Begin evacuation.	Everyone should evacuate the building immediately upon hearing the alarm. Prearranged evacuation routes should be used.
Maintain orderly movement.	Do not permit individuals to stop for coats, books, or other belongings. Individuals should walk quietly and be supervised. If the designated route is blocked, the next nearest exit or designated alternate route should be used. Designated staff or volunteers should stand at doors until everyone in the room or area has filed out, and should then take rosters and emergency kits.
Maintain accountability.	When the assembly areas are reached, designated staff or volunteers should ensure everyone is accounted for. Discrepancies need to be reported.
Remain in assigned area.	Keep all individuals in the assigned assembly area, until instructions are given.
Record evacuation times.	
Issue return to building notification.	All individuals return to building in an orderly, safe manner.

Adapted from: The Virginia Educator's Guide for Planning and Conducting School Emergency Drills,
http://www.dcjs.virginia.gov/vcss/documents/educatorsGuideForDrills.pdf

Evacuation Drill Checklist

	Action	Comments/Notes
	911 notified	
	Drill information sent to parents/guardians	
	All individuals evacuating remained quiet and orderly	

Staff or volunteers closed doors as they left (kept unlocked)	
Restrooms and hallways cleared	
Radio communication effective	
Emergency kit brought to assembly area	
Proper accounting for individuals conducted	
Alarm notification heard in all areas	
Assembly area clearly marked, safe, and effective for the evacuation	
Evacuation times recorded	

Adapted from: Lincoln County Schools Drill Evaluation Form,
http://rems.ed.gov/docs/repository/REMS_000067_0001.pdf

Lockdown Drill Procedures

Before the Drill Date	
Review lockdown procedures with staff, volunteers, members, students.	The key to a successful drill is awareness of the drill goals and objectives and understanding of roles and responsibilities.
Announce the drill date to staff and volunteers.	
Send a letter to parents/guardians.	Let parents know that emergency preparedness is necessary and that it is essential that they take it seriously.
Day of the Drill	
Notify 911 dispatchers of the drill.	Also, notify them of the conclusion of the drill.
Assemble the crisis team and/or designated evaluators.	The crisis team members and/or designated evaluators should be assigned sections of the building to evaluate.
Initiate lockdown	Follow the lockdown procedures in your emergency plan.
Evaluate each room.	Evaluators should knock on doors, listen for talking, look in windows for visible individuals, check for computer monitors left on.

| Issue a release. | Once the proper procedure is used, issue a release. Only staff need to know the proper procedure for release. |
| Evaluate and debrief. | Use the lockdown drill checklist for the evaluation. |

Adapted from: The Virginia Educator's Guide for Planning and Conducting School Emergency Drills,
http://www.dcjs.virginia.gov/vcss/documents/educatorsGuideForDrills.pdf

Lockdown Drill Checklist

	Action	Comments/Notes
	911 notified	
	Drill information sent to parents/guardians	
	Scenario reviewed with staff and volunteers in advance	
	Staff, volunteers, students, and members went into a room, closed and locked all doors and windows	
	Computer monitors turned off	
	Individuals in rooms were quiet	
	Signs placed on doors to indicate lockdown	
	Process to account for all individuals conducted	
	Drapes, curtains, blinds closed	
	Release notification successfully issued	

Adapted from: The Virginia Educator's Guide for Planning and Conducting School Emergency Drills,
http://www.dcjs.virginia.gov/vcss/documents/educatorsGuideForDrills.pdf

Keeping Drills Realistic and Unpredictable

Emergency situations may occur at any time during the day or year. It is beneficial to conduct drills in ways that reflect this variability. Make the drills realistic, but do so safely. For example, vary the times and conditions for drills, to include:

- Class or service changes.
- Recess, gym classes, social hours, events, and meetings.
- Arrival and dismissal times.
- Times when food service areas are occupied.
- After hours (i.e., dances, theater, athletic events, community functions).

Ideas for Conducting Realistic Drills

- During an evacuation drill, block normal routes or use human "blockers."
- Remove individuals during a drill to see how long it takes to notice and act.
- Remove a staff member (unannounced) from his/her group to see if individuals in the group can follow procedures on their own.
- Conduct drills as people arrive in the morning or around dismissal time. Identify unique issues that arise during these times.
- Conduct spontaneous drills with specific groups—for instance, to see how quickly a room can go into lockdown mode.

Communicating About Drills

Drills and other exercises are about learning and improving. Exercises can be used to reinforce a positive message about security and preparedness.

To underscore this message and keep from alarming participants and the community:

- At the beginning of each year or season, outline the different exercises that will be held.
- Notify households and caregivers anytime you plan a drill for your facility. Do not let them be caught unawares!
- When appropriate, use signage or other means to inform the community that an exercise is in progress.

Frequency and Timing

Your organization may have requirements for how often drills are conducted. Regardless of requirements, drill scenarios should be practiced regularly to ensure that staff, trained volunteers, and building occupants are prepared to remain as safe as possible during potentially dangerous events.

Drills and other exercises should be conducted at least annually, and whenever procedures are developed or revised.

Using Tabletop Exercises

Tabletop exercises:

- Can range from simple to complex and are usually focused on strategic, policy-oriented issues.
- Can be used to introduce community partners to new plans and procedures in the context of a specific scenario.
- Allow for informal and in-depth discussion and slow-paced problem solving. For example, the participants might review an actual event that happened elsewhere and discuss, What if that happened here?
- Help to identify potential challenges and identify solutions.
- Provide information to help you update or improve your plan.

Examples of Tabletop Exercises

Tabletop Scenario K-12 School

Scenario: It is Valentine's Day just around lunchtime. A young man appears at your entry area with a large bouquet of flowers and states he has a delivery for a teacher. The front office staff buzz the individual into the front office. As he approaches the front office, a custodian thinks he sees the individual carrying a gun.

Answer the following question: What should the custodian, other staff, and teachers do?

Scenario Update 1: Before the custodian can take any action, the individual drops the flowers and pulls out a gun. There are students in the hallways headed toward the cafeteria while others remain in their classrooms.

Answer the following questions:

- What are the priority actions?
- Who will be in charge?
- What information should be communicated? How will this information be communicated? And who do you need to communicate with?

Scenario Update 2: The gunman fires the gun and then runs toward the cafeteria. Five students and the custodian have been critically wounded. In addition, there are numerous other students who were injured as they ran away from the gunfire. Teachers are trying to account for the students who were in the hallways. There is confusion about the gunman's whereabouts. Law enforcement officers and first responders have arrived at the scene. They have cordoned off the surrounding area and are preventing parents and guardians from getting to where their children are located. The school and immediate neighbors are locked down. The media has converged on the scene.

Answer the following questions:

- What are the priority actions?
- What do you need to do to protect and comfort students?
- What support can you give to the law enforcement officers?
- How will you interface with the media?

Scenario Update 3: Thirty (30) minutes later, officers apprehend the gunman in the neighborhood surrounding the school. Parents are anxious to be reunited with their children. The media is continuing to broadcast information from the scene.

Answer the following questions:

- What are the immediate recovery actions (e.g., reunification, counseling, etc.)?
- What are the longer-term recovery needs?
- How prepared is your school to deal with an event like this?
- How prepared is your school to interface with local law enforcement agencies?

Tabletop Scenario Institution of Higher Education

Scenario: It is a Friday night, just prior to the week of final examinations. A basketball game is in progress with a rival school. Campus police officers are providing security at the game. There is another patrol officer on campus completing normal, routine patrol duties. The college president sometimes attends the games, but she is out of town on college business.

The team has done well this season but is expecting a challenge from this competitor. The gymnasium is filled to capacity, and the crowd is becoming rowdy. In the days leading up to the game, there have been some nasty exchanges between the rivals on social media sites.

Answer the following question: What, if any, are the potential concerns?

Scenario Update 1: It is near half-time. The home team has done well throughout the first half, but it's still considered anybody's game. Suddenly, a disturbance breaks out in the middle of the seating area, near the bottom of the stands. Several loud pops are heard, which sound like gunfire. The crowd panics and bolts.

The officers are unable to reach the area of the disturbance. One officer observes what he thinks is the suspect, running away from the gymnasium toward a campus residential area.

When an officer reaches the area of the disturbance, he discovers that a student has been struck by an apparent stray bullet. The student appears to be critically wounded. In addition, there are numerous other people who were injured as the crowd pushed out of the gymnasium.

Answer the following questions:

- What are the priority actions?
- Who will be in charge?
- What information should be communicated? How will this information be communicated? And who do you need to communicate with?

Scenario Update 2: The campus patrol officer requests assistance from the County Sheriff's Office to start a search for the suspect at the main campus and to help identify witnesses in the crowd that is still milling about near the gymnasium.

The college gymnasium is now a crime scene and is closed to all except law enforcement investigators and responding emergency medical personnel. The perpetrator has not been apprehended. Some members of the crowd identified the individual as a student who is being investigated for alleged plagiarism. The media have begun to arrive.

Answer the following questions:

- What are the priority actions?

- How will you manage the media interest in the scene?

Scenario Update 3: Two hours later, the gunman has been shot by law enforcement officers and the area has been secured. You have multiple injured students, staff, and faculty. The media, parents, and local citizens are converging on your campus.

Answer the following questions:

- What are the immediate recovery actions (e.g., reunification, counseling, etc.)?
- What are the longer term recovery needs?
- How prepared is your college or university to deal with an event like this?
- How prepared is your college or university to interface with local law enforcement agencies?

Adapted from: Texas School Safety Center, Texas State University, Higher Education Services, Active Shooter/Killer Multiple Target Locations Exercise Tabletop, http://www.txssc.txstate.edu/HE/tabletop#Exer2

Tabletop Scenario House of Worship

Scenario: It is a warm, sunny day. As the service is just about to end, a man gets out of his car wearing a long raincoat, walks past two greeters without acknowledging them, and enters the worship area. The individual is unfamiliar to the greeters. As he enters, one of the greeters says to the other one, "Do you see a gun under his raincoat?"

Answer the following question: What should the greeters do?

Scenario Update 1: Before the greeters take any action, the individual pulls out a gun. There are children in classrooms and a nursery in other parts of the building. Also, there are volunteers setting up for the post-service reception.

Answer the following questions:

- What are the priority actions?
- Who will be in charge?

- What information should be communicated? How will this information be communicated? And who do you need to communicate with?

Scenario Update 2: The gunman fires the gun and runs out of the sanctuary. One person has been struck by an apparent stray bullet and is critically wounded. In addition, there are numerous other people who were injured as the crowd pushed out of the sanctuary. Parents and guardians are anxious about their children who are in classrooms in another section of the building. There is confusion about the gunman's whereabouts. Law enforcement officers and first responders have arrived at the scene. They have cordoned off the surrounding area and are preventing people from getting to where their children are located. Also, they have instructed the congregation and immediate neighbors to shelter-in-place. The media has converged on the scene.

Answer the following questions:

- What are the priority actions?
- What do you need to do to protect and comfort congregation members?
- What support can you give to the law enforcement officers?
- How will you interface with the media?

Scenario Update 3: Thirty (30) minutes later, officers apprehend the gunman in the neighborhood surrounding the house of worship. Parents are anxious to be reunited with their children. The media is continuing to broadcast information from the scene.

Answer the following questions:

- What are the immediate recovery actions (e.g., reunification, counseling, etc.)?
- What are the longer-term recovery needs?
- How prepared is your house of worship to deal with an event like this?
- How prepared is your house of worship to interface with local law enforcement agencies?

After-Action Findings and Corrective Actions

Exercises are a means of learning what works and what does not work as planned. To gain the benefit of each exercise, the team should conduct an after-action review to analyze lessons learned.

- Conduct a post-exercise evaluation immediately after the exercise.

- Include everyone who participated in the exercise.
- Assess whether the exercise's objectives were achieved.
- Discuss the positive and negative outcomes.
- Allow time for participants to discuss their observations.
- Create an after-action report with steps for improvement.

Questions for the After-Action Review of a Drill

- How long did the drill take?
- Who designed the drill?
- What worked well?
- What needs to be improved?
- Do any other people need to be added to your team?
- What would the emergency response time be if this were not a drill?
- What should be our next steps?
- How will we track completion of the improvement steps?

Updating the Plan

Effective plans are never finished. They can always be updated based on experience, research, and changing vulnerabilities. Community stakeholders and experts should be included in the updating process. At a minimum, plans and procedures should be updated:

- At least annually.
- Following drills or other exercises.
- After an incident.

As with all planning and implementation initiatives, there is a danger that enthusiasm will wane as time passes. An annual review and update process is a way to combat this problem and renew enthusiasm for a vigorous emergency management program.

Resources

You can use the following resources to learn more about communicating and exercising plans.

Online resources:

- Emergency Exercises: An Effective Way to Validate Emergency Management Plans. *ERCMExpress.*
- Planning and Conducting a Functional Exercise. *Helpful Hints for School Emergency Management.*

- <u>Sample Security Drill Law Guidance and Resources.</u> New Jersey Department of Education.
- <u>School Tabletops, Drills, and Exercises.</u> U.S. Department of Education.
- <u>The Virginia Educator's Guide for Planning and Conducting School Emergency Drills.</u> VA Department of Criminal Justice Services, VA Center for School Safety, and VA Department of Education.
- <u>Resource site for E/L361 Course</u>: Exercises and Drills Resources.
- <u>Homeland Security Exercise and Evaluation Program (HSEEP).</u>

Training:

- <u>IS-120: An Introduction to Exercises</u>
- <u>IS-130: Exercise Evaluation and Improvement Planning</u>
- <u>IS-139: Exercise Design</u>
- <u>E/L104: Exercise Design</u>
- <u>E/L361: Multihazard Emergency Planning for Schools</u>

Lesson Summary

You should now understand how to stay prepared by communicating and exercising your plan.

The next lesson will present a review of key concepts covered in the entire course and provide an opportunity for you to assess your learning and provide feedback.

www.ingramcontent.com/pod-product-compliance
Lightning Source LLC
Chambersburg PA
CBHW081305250726

48662CB00008B/2407